Presented To:

From:

Date:

ETZ CHAIM: TREE OF LIFE

FOREWORD BY JONATHAN BERNIS

ETZ CHAIM: TREE OF LIFE

Lessons Learned from the Tree of Life

MESSIANIC RABBI
ERIC E. WALKER

DESTINY IMAGE® PUBLISHERS, INC.

P.O. Box 310, Shippensburg, PA 17257-0310

"Promoting Inspired Lives."

This book and all other Destiny Image, Revival Press, MercyPlace, Fresh Bread, Destiny Image Fiction, and Treasure House books are available at Christian bookstores and distributors worldwide.

For a U.S. bookstore nearest you, call 1-800-722-6774.

For more information on foreign distributors, call 717-532-3040.

Reach us on the Internet: www.destinyimage.com.

ISBN 13 TP: 978-0-7684-4124-6

ISBN 13 EBook: 978-0-7684-8837-1

For Worldwide Distribution, Printed in the U.S.A.

2 3 4 5 6 7 / 16 15 14 13 12

DEDICATION

To my incredible wife, Lora, whom I adore and who has labored side by side with me on this project. G-D has blessed me with a Proverbs 31 woman.

To our precious children: Amanda, Skylar, and Kenzie, and our precious granddaughter, Chloe! May they follow Yeshua with all their hearts, souls, and minds and love Him with all their hearts.

And in loving memory of Robert and Lillian Amper, who instilled in me a love of Israel and my rich Jewish heritage.

ACKNOWLEDGMENTS

THERE IS NO GREATER contributor to this book than the G-D of Abraham, Isaac, and Jacob, who redeemed me from a life serving the world and gave me a gift so great that my life would be forever changed: Yeshua ha Mashiach—He deserves all the praise, honor, and glory.

This book is a testimony to the love and prayerful support of many who have sown into my life. I have been privileged to sit under great teaching and want to thank those who have made an outstanding contribution to me in my walk with the Lord.

FAMILY

My wife, Lora, and our children, Skylar and Amanda, who have shared this journey with me and have been the greatest encouragers. Their love and support are treasures and gifts from G-D.

My mother, Iris Walker, and my late father, Herbert Walker, who equipped me to accomplish anything I believed in. Without that foundation, there would be nothing to build on.

My beloved late grandparents, Robert and Lillian Amper, who instilled in me a love of Israel and my Jewish heritage. Their vision, love, and support of Israel are as alive today as they were at those Shabbat, Holiday, and Israel Bond dinners in McKeesport in the 1960s and '70s.

MENTORS AND TEACHERS

Rabbi Robert Solomon and Dorothy Solomon, who took me from being on fire for the world and groomed, trained, counseled, and corrected me—and ignited in me a fire for the Lord that cannot be quenched. Thank you!

Don Smith, whose commitment to the truth of the Bible has taught me and inspired me since the day we met.

CONTRIBUTORS

Karie Mitchell Photography for catching the vision and making extraordinary photographs through the eye of G-D!

Mark and Daniah Greenberg and the entire TLV team for their vision and support to bring the truth to life.

Destiny Image Publishers, that possesses a unique heart for this work to go forth and a heart for the restoration of Israel, both physically and spiritually.

MISHPACHA

The love, support, and encouragement from Congregation Beth Hallel in Birmingham, Alabama, have motivated me to boldly step out in faith and write this book. Thanks to them for their prayer support and encouragement. Thanks to my mishpacha, who allows me to teach and to lead; and a special thanks for their support as I strive for more of Him in my life.

And thank you, dear reader, for allowing this book's influence in your life. May your walk be strengthened and deepened even a little as you walk through this text and as we take this journey together.

ENDORSEMENTS

Rabbi Eric Walker's *Etz Chaim: Tree of Life* is a masterful design for Messianic discipleship and Spirit-controlled living. Rabbi Walker's step-by-step approach to living the sanctified life includes his ingenious use of botany interwoven with childhood experiences and highly practical applications of solid biblical truth. His simple and effective self-checklists at the end of each carefully laid out and expounded precept allows the serious disciple to calculate exactly an individualized appropriate course of action. Rabbi Walker's extensive use of Scripture is ideal for all, but most especially for those disciples newer to the Word of God. Whether for use in a discipleship course for one or a group, a home Bible study, or a preaching series, I wholeheartedly commend *Etz Chaim: Tree of Life* to anyone engaged in Kingdom living.

RAYMOND L. GANNON, PhD
The King's University Dean of Messianic Jewish Studies
Academic Dean of the Jewish Voice Messianic Career Institute

Only a Messianic Rabbi who is flooded with G-D's Spirit can teach the end-time understanding of the Torah. Feast on the heart of G-D as Rabbi Eric Walker unfolds this end-time revelation.

SID ROTH
Host, *It's Supernatural!* Television
www.SidRoth.org

In *Etz Chaim,* Rabbi Eric Walker takes readers back to the dawn of human history and then to our own modern story. Those who are game to reconsider the ancient "Tree of Life" and the "Garden of Eden," along with the more liturgical employment of the "Tree of Life" in the synagogue's liturgy, will get something for their own lives through Rabbi Walker's unpacking of the ancient and modern parable of the tree. I am happy to recommend his insightful and inspirational book.

DR. JEFFREY L. SEIF

Etz Chaim: Tree of Life is a book that I will put on our "must read" list at our Shoresh David Messianic Synagogues. First, I loved the parable that G-D gave to Rabbi Walker; it is a great foundation for the book. I thought the Scriptures used were extremely insightful as we journeyed into the intricacies of the Tree and its spiritual components. But what makes it extra special for me is that this book takes the spiritual understanding in each chapter and develops key life applications. You can't read this book without learning how to walk more closely with G-D.

RABBI STEVEN J. WEILER
Senior Rabbi, Shoresh David Messianic Synagogue,
Executive officer of the Messianic Jewish Bible Project

With the voice of "everyman," Rabbi Walker provides an insightful and thoughtful look into the deeper roots of our faith in Messiah Yeshua (Jesus). From the roots nourished in rich soil to the top branches that reach in praise to its Maker, *Etz Chaim: Tree of Life* will not only provide those insights, but also draw us closer to the Creator.

Terri Gillespie
Author, *Making Eye Contact With G-D*,
and "Restoration of Israel Minute," heard internationally

Amazingly, the biblical Tree of Life, which was so central to our earliest beginnings, has seldom been examined. Eric Walker's approach of parable and analogy help us to plumb the depth of its meaning. Among his associates, he is known as an original thinker who has unusual insight.

PAUL LIBERMAN
President, Messianic Jewish Alliance of America
Author, *The Fig Tree Blossoms*

Rabbi Eric Walker firmly believes in bending the knee to biblical authority, and *Etz Chaim: Tree of Life* is an outpouring of this conviction. Using the richness of his Jewish roots, he builds precept upon precept and reveals the beauty in the Tree of Life, which truly waters the heart and renews the soul. Rabbi Walker is a powerful voice in the growing Messianic Jewish community, and this contribution is a potent volley for the advancing Kingdom of Messiah.

Darek Isaacs
President, Watchmen 33
Author, *Can G-d Create a Rock So Big He Can't Move It?*

CONTENTS

FOREWORD 19

PROLOGUE. 21

INTRODUCTION. 27

Chapter 1

THE GROUND. 33

    Seven Lessons Learned From the Ground. 41

    Plowing 43

    Ground Breaking 44

Chapter 2

THE SEEDS. 49

    Seven Lessons Learned From the Seeds 58

    Sowing New Seeds 60

    Sowing Good Seeds. 61

Chapter 3

THE ROOTS 67

    Seven Lessons Learned From the Roots. 76

    Beneath the Surface 79

    Growing Deeper. 81

Chapter 4

    THE TRUNK 87

        Seven Lessons Learned From the Trunk 95

        Main Frame 97

        Body Building 99

Chapter 5

    THE BRANCHES 105

        Seven Lessons Learned From the Branches 115

        Out on a Limb 117

        Branching Out 119

Chapter 6

    THE LEAVES 125

        Seven Lessons Learned From the Leaves 130

        Letting Go 133

        Bursting Forth 134

Chapter 7

    THE FRUIT 141

        Seven Lessons Learned From the Fruit 147

        The Harvest 150

        Bearing Fruit 153

    EPILOGUE 159

    CLOSING PRAYER 169

    GLOSSARY 171

FOREWORD

MESSIANIC RABBI ERIC WALKER's brilliantly transparent exploration of biblical wisdom and how he learned to apply it to his own life is a beautifully balanced study of the familiar yet enigmatic subject of wisdom and knowledge from the Tree of Life, first mentioned in Genesis 2. Wisdom literature of the Bible is exciting because it teaches us how to incorporate biblical perspective in dealing with real life in real time, with all of its myriad challenges.

His comparison of the events of our lives to trees that adjust to the changing seasons provides an in-depth explanation of maturing on the outside while the earth from which we all came protects the roots of our very being—keeping us stable and strong in the face of adversity.

This book brings to life the biblical journey all believers must take who desire to hear the words of Messiah, "Well done, good and faithful servant!" when we meet Him face to face.

Read this powerful book and allow it to enhance and bless your life experience in a variety of ways you have yet to imagine. As Eric himself says, "May it shape and transform you more into the image of Messiah and His calling on your life."

MESSIANIC RABBI JONATHAN BERNIS
President and CEO, Jewish Voice Ministries International
Phoenix, Arizona

PROLOGUE

W HAT YOU ARE READING and are about to encounter are excerpts from my life experiences and revelations from the Lord, intertwined with a parable about a tree that grew into a sermon series and then matured into this book. May it shape and transform you more into the image of Messiah and His calling on your life.

This book grew out of a sermon series, and like so much revelation from the Lord, it too has taken on a life of its own. G-D gave me a parable. "A parable?" you say. Yes, I knew about parables as a Jewish method of teaching and understood why it was Yeshua's preferred teaching method. But G-D had never given me a parable before, so I didn't really understand what it was until I wrote out the words of this parable, read it, prayed and then re-read it, and searched the Scriptures for its hidden meaning. The words are very carefully chosen, as they always are by G-D, and lined up perfectly with His Word. And He said:

> The children of the Kingdom of G-D are like the trees
> where the seasons change the outward appearance, but
> the root never changes. In its season, people gaze upon

21

the buds and marvel at the branches. In its season, the colors like Joseph's robe burst forth, and people stand in awe. And winter comes, and the trees shed their beautiful leaves, and their outward appearance becomes bleak and barren. There's no longer any interest in the tree. But beneath the surface, the root grows deeper—yet no one sees.

And so the journey to understanding the hidden meaning of this parable began with a deep dive into the Word of G-D. Since any journey begins with a first step, I opened my Bible to Genesis 1:1 and began to search for the meaning behind the parable. It didn't take all that long, and I found it right away in the second chapter of the story of creation where we are introduced to the two trees.

Let's begin with Genesis 2:8-10:

> Now the Lord G-D had planted a garden in the east, in Eden; and there He put the man He had formed. And the Lord G-D made all kinds of trees grow out of the ground—trees that were pleasing to the eye and good for food. In the middle of the garden were the tree of life and the tree of the knowledge of good and evil.
>
> A river watering the garden flowed from Eden; from there it was separated into four headwaters....

And pick it up in verse 15:

> The Lord G-D took the man and put him in the Garden of Eden to work it and take care of it. And the Lord G-D commanded the man, "You are free to eat from any tree in the garden; but you must not eat from the tree of the

knowledge of good and evil, for when you eat of it you will surely die" (Gen. 2:15-17).

What is this Tree of the Knowledge of Good and Evil? It represents our thoughts, our mind, and our understanding; by its fruit we are able to walk by sight. The fruit of the Tree of Knowledge fuels our ability to know about G-D and to know about the enemy, the accuser of the body of believers. It is the fruit of the Tree of the Knowledge of Good and Evil that gives us insight into the clear separation of good and evil that was alluded to in Genesis 1, where G-D separated the light from the dark and called the light good. Through this Tree we are able to recognize good and evil, but we are still left to our own choices as to which we will follow.

Back in the Genesis 1 Garden, we find a second tree. It is the Tree of Life, the *Etz Chaim.* Eating from it is the key to immortality, eternal life, and eternal relationship with G-D. Since it was sin that separated us from G-D and cost us eternal life, it is clear that eternal life also carried with it the eternal relationship with G-D. Its fruit is the Holy Spirit *(Ruach HaKodesh)* of G-D. This Tree's fruit takes us past knowledge and into faith. As Second Corinthians 5:7 states, *"For we walk by faith, not by sight,."* In order to do this, we must eat of its fruit; but because of man's disobedience, its fruit has been denied us.

There is a key to understanding the Word of G-D, and the key is wisdom. Wisdom allows us to discern the clues G-D gives us and unravel the many mysteries contained therein. King Solomon wrote this about wisdom in Proverbs 3:13-18:

> *Blessed is the man who finds wisdom, the man who gains understanding, for she is more profitable than silver and yields better returns than gold. She is more precious than rubies; nothing you desire can compare with her. Long life*

*is in her right hand; in her left hand are riches and honor.
Her ways are pleasant ways, and all her paths are peace.
She is a tree of life to those who embrace her; those who lay
hold of her will be blessed.*

In Judaism, the Torah scrolls (the first five books of the Bible)
are usually wrapped around wooden poles, which are also called
Etz Chaim, a Tree of Life. Is it because they are wooden like the
tree that they bear this name, or is it because what is wrapped
upon them is the wisdom that King Solomon referenced? It is the
Word that is the Tree of Life—not the scroll, not the pole, but the
Tree of Life that G-D was talking about in His Word.

It is through this passage of Scripture that we understand that
the Word is living. *"In the beginning was the Word. The Word was
with G-D, and the Word was G-D"* (John 1:1). This living Word was
conveyed to us in the *Tanakh*, the Hebrew Bible, through Moses,
the prophets, and the other contributors to the text. In the *B'rit
Hadasha*, we are introduced to the Living Word in Messiah Yeshua.
His words revealed the fulfillment of G-D's plan of atonement.
He revealed that the secret to eternal life was through faith in
Messiah Yeshua. It was through the ultimate sacrifice of this Man
who hung on a Tree that we have eternal life.

Who knew? Something as simple and as common as a tree held
so much meaning that it was difficult to fathom. I had so many
questions! Did the kind of tree matter? Could it be a fig tree or an
olive tree since they were both so prominent in the Bible? Or was
there a lesson in every tree? What about the parts of the tree? Was
there something hidden within each part? There is the seed, the
roots, the trunk, the branches, the leaves, and the fruit. You have
the air, sun, rain, and dirt that all affect the tree. And, in the final
analysis, every one of these influences will have an impact on the
growth and maturity of the tree.

G-D did not give me this parable and this sermon series for my own information. There was a purpose to all that He was showing me. There was a message here for me to share with you. Contained within was a supernatural recipe that, when mixed together and prepared according to His plan, would give us insight into the *Lev Elohim*—The Heart of G-D.

In Jewish numerology, the number seven is the number of completion and refers to the days of creation. It is no accident that the contents of this book are broken down into sevens. There are seven lessons from the tree broken down into seven parts with seven exercises at the end of each part. This is how it was given to me and how it is being given to you.

May the Lord bless you with new wisdom, insight, and understanding as you read *Etz Chaim: Tree of Life.*

INTRODUCTION

*Now the Lord G-D had planted a garden in the east, in Eden; and there He put the man He had formed. And the Lord G-D made all kinds of trees grow out of the ground— trees that were pleasing to the eye and good for food. In the middle of the garden were the **tree of life** and the tree of the knowledge of good and evil* (Gen. 2:8-9).

HAVE YOU EVER WONDERED why this tree, that was so impor- tant to G-D, seems to have disappeared from our sight? Or why no one can seem to pinpoint the exact location of the Garden of Eden? Ah, the consequences of disobedience! Adam, oh Adam, what have you done?

…"The man has now become like one of Us, knowing good and evil. He must not be allowed to reach out his hand and take also from the tree of life and eat, and live forever." So the Lord G-D banished him from the Garden of Eden to work the ground from which he had been taken. After He drove the man out, He placed on the east side of the Garden

of Eden cherubim and a flaming sword flashing back and forth to guard the way to the tree of life (Gen. 3:22-24).

Has G-D really cut us off from the Tree of Life? Was our disobedience and separation from G-D to be a permanent condition? Or could it be that the Scriptures give us the real clue when it goes on to tell us that the way is guarded? If it is guarded, is there a way in? Is there a password? If the way is guarded, is the guard a man? And if it is a man, could that man be the promised Jewish Messiah who holds the key to eternal life? John 3:16 says, *"For G-D so loved the world that He gave His one and only Son, that whoever believes in Him shall not perish but have eternal life."*

As we fast forward to the end of G-D's Word, we see that we have something to overcome in order to eat from the *Etz Chaim*, the Tree of Life. Revelation 2:7 says, *"He who has an ear, let him hear what the Spirit is saying to Messiah's communities. To the one who overcomes, I will grant the right to eat from the **Tree of Life**, which is in the Paradise of G-D."*

The Hebrew words *Etz Chaim* translate to "tree of life" and are referred to in Proverbs 3:13-18:

> *Blessed is the man who finds wisdom, the man who gains understanding, for she is more profitable than silver and yields better returns than gold. She is more precious than rubies; nothing you desire can compare with her. Long life is in her right hand; in her left hand are riches and honor. Her ways are pleasant ways, and all her paths are peace. She is a tree of life* [Etz Chaim] *to those who embrace her; those who lay hold of her will be blessed.*

In both non-Messianic and Messianic Jewish Synagogues, the *Etz Chaim* is the name and the first words of a liturgical chant sung while the Torah is held up. Many will point at the Torah as it is held high for all to see. The words from this chant that follow demonstrate that the Torah represents the Tree of Life— G-D's Word!

ETZ CHAYIM	TREE OF LIFE
Etz chaim hi lamachazikim ba, Vetomecheha me-ushar.	A tree of life to those who hold fast to it, and all who cling to it find happiness.
Deracheha—d'rechei no-am, Vechol netivotecha shalom... Hashiveinu Adonai eilecha v'nashuva Chadeish chadeish yameinu Chadeish yameinu k'kedem...	Its ways are ways of pleasantness, and all its paths are peace. Help us and guide us, inspire us and provide us with the wisdom Your Torah can show. Cause us to learn, renew, and return, just as in days of old.

In nature, there are over 400 billion trees on Earth. Something that numerous and that common may hold the key to a deeper understanding of G-D's Word. G-D uses the things of the natural to reveal to us the supernatural.

My wife, Lora, and I were on a flight to the Annual Messiah Conference in Grantham, Pennsylvania, and I was in prayer about what the Lord would have me preach on when I returned from the conference. I began drawing in my notebook, and the sketch became a clear picture of roots. I began to contemplate the roots and jotted down a number of notes related to roots. I was sure that the message was about roots! But the Lord had another plan. While I was in class, I was looking out the window, and in my spirit the Lord spoke to me and gave me this parable:

The children of the Kingdom of G-D are like the trees where the seasons change the outward appearance, but the root never changes. In its season, people gaze upon the buds and marvel at the branches. In its season, the colors like Joseph's robe burst forth, and people stand in awe. And winter comes, and the trees shed their beautiful leaves, and their outward appearance becomes bleak and barren. There's no longer any interest in the tree. But beneath the surface, the root grows deeper—yet no one sees.

This is the parable that set in motion the sermon series and this book, *Etz Chaim: Tree of Life*. The pages that follow take you on a journey to revealing G-D's Word through each part of the tree—beginning with the dirt. Yes, the dirt! Why start with the dirt? I asked the same question and G-D's answer was, "Because I did!" Our exploration will take us deep into the roots, through the seed, up the trunk, out to the branches, down to the leaves, and culminate with the fruit.

THE
GROUND

Chapter 1

THE GROUND

THE PHRASE "IN THE beginning" evokes a knowing nod from all who have heard or read those words. We associate those very words to the opening of the Book of Genesis. As in all of life, there is a beginning, so too this book has its beginning. In the Introduction I shared the question I asked as I was searching for a starting point for the sermon series that led to this book. That question was, "Lord, where do You want me to start?" Some would say I heard the answer in my spirit, and others would say I heard an audible voice. All I know is I heard the words, "Start with the dirt." Since I was already having a conversation with G-D, I did not hesitate to ask the obvious question, "Why start with the dirt?" I should not have been surprised by the answer, but I was when I heard, "Because I did."

We serve a G-D of order, and He reveals to us in the natural what He wants us to see in the supernatural. Our origin has a genesis, a beginning. The dirt, the dust, the ground itself is the very place that man began. In Genesis 2:7, we read, *"The Lord G-D formed the man from the dust of the ground and breathed into his nostrils the breath of life, and the man became a living being."* Adam's name in Hebrew means earth and has become a generic term for man. The dust of the earth is not only our beginning, in the end it is also our final, fleshly state. We return to our original state, back to the dirt, to become part of the land.

I have been blessed over the past two years to have had many in-depth conversations with a man whose credentials in science are as long as my arm. He has dedicated his life to the pursuit of new medical technologies and breakthrough science. Our conversations have ranged from the origins of life to brain activity after the heart stops. It was during these conversations that we began to discuss creation and the science of genetics and the building blocks of life. In preparation for this chapter, I asked my friend to write to me the answer to these questions:

1. Do all living creatures share a common element or elements in their DNA that would support that all is made from the dust of the earth?

2. If so, what and how many commonalities are there?

3. Would the common elements from the dust of the earth be enough to assign the label to the dust of the earth as the fundamental building block?

According to Dr. Donald H. Marks, noted author, patent holder, and a Messianic Jewish member of Congregation Beth Hallel in Birmingham, Alabama:

All living creatures on earth share a common set of molecules, which are the nucleic acids (DNA & RNA), protein, carbohydrates and lipids. All the molecules including DNA are made up from a few common elements: carbon, oxygen, hydrogen, nitrogen, and phosphorous. Lesser component elements include potassium, calcium, selenium, sulfur and traces of others. All these elements are found in the earth, and in the air. Oxygen, hydrogen, and nitrogen are gases in the air that are also found in the ground, particularly in living and decaying organic waste. These gases are also trapped in minerals and dissolved in the water. I think that contemporary people may think of dust as simply loose dirt, but in the Bible, the dust of the earth is a reference to dry ground, not to dirt. In the biblical sense, the dust of the earth does therefore, refer in general to the ground that we live on and in, and from whose components all creatures are made. When it is written that we come from and return to the dust of the earth, it is in recognition that all creatures are composed physically of the same chemical elements of the earth. Since all living creatures come from the same dust of the earth, by implication all of life is composed of the same common chemical elements. The Bible states this, and we now know this to be true in a biochemical sense.[1]

Just as in agriculture, the ground must be prepared in a certain way to obtain the highest yield, so too our hearts are the fertile ground that must be prepared properly for the Word of G-D to take hold. In Genesis 1:11, G-D said, *"Let the land produce vegetation."* It's the land that produces the vegetation; it's the land, the earth, the ground itself that produces the vegetation: *"Plants bearing seed according to their kinds and trees bearing fruit with seed in it according to their kinds. And G-D saw that it was good"* (Gen. 1:12).

Genesis 2:4-7 tells us:

...When the Lord made the earth and the heavens—and no shrub of the field had yet appeared on the earth and no plant of the field had yet sprung up, for the Lord G-D had not sent rain on the earth and there was no man to work the ground, but streams came up from the earth and watered the whole surface of the ground—the Lord G-D formed the man from the dust of the ground and breathed into his nostrils the breath of life, and the man became a living being.

From dust of the earth we came; from dust of the earth will we return. Dry land cannot sustain life. It requires water to soften it and break up the hard places. Because our fundamental building material is dust, we are natural beings, but we are also spiritual created in the image of G-D. We, like G-D, are two parts invisible and one part visible. In the same way that our physical being needs nourishment and water to survive, our spiritual entities need sustenance to grow and to flourish. If we remain spiritually dry, we have no shape or form and little function in G-D's Kingdom. If we add the living water, the Word, we can be molded and shaped. Once we add the living water, it is easier to separate the rocky, hard places from the more formable material. Unless we, like the dirt, are sifted, our lives will be filled with rocky places. But, with sifting and refinement, we are transformed from rough concrete aggregate into beautiful porcelain powder. Both are made up of dirt, but the preparation, refinement, and forming transforms them from raw and rough into beautiful vessels.

The dirt, the land itself, was clearly identified in various passages of the Bible as being one of the essential elements to the survival of G-D's chosen people. We read in Numbers 13:17-20:

> *When Moses sent them to explore Canaan, he said, "Go up through the Negev and on into the hill country. See what the land is like and whether the people who live there are strong or weak, few or many. What kind of land do they live in? Is it good or bad? What kind of towns do they live in? Are they unwalled or fortified? How is the soil? Is it fertile or poor? Are there trees on it or not? Do your best to bring back some of the fruit of the land...."*

Here is what he was saying to them, "Go look at the land. Go look at the dirt. Go look at the ground. Go to the basics. Go right back to this building block of life that you were formed from and check it out. Don't just look at the buildings. Don't just look at their dwelling places. Don't just look at their schools. Don't just look at what they're doing or how big they are. Look at their land and see whether it's fertile. See whether it can support life." Our natural tendency is to be distracted by the size of the people and how strong and well-armed they are, but G-D was leading them into a Promised *Land*, and it was the land that would sustain life.

The role of the soil is fundamental to growth. The Jewish prophet Isaiah makes this clear in Isaiah 61:11, *"For as the soil makes the sprout come up and a garden causes seeds to grow, so the Sovereign Lord will make righteousness and praise spring up before all nations."*

In the New Covenant Scriptures, the *B'rit Hadasha*, we see that the reference point of Jewish life is agricultural. As the Messiah taught, He employed the age-old method of teaching using parables, which contained both practical and spiritual truths. Hidden within His references to the natural elements of life were keys to understanding the mysteries of the supernatural realm.

Let's examine one of Messiah's parables from Matthew 13:3-23:

And He told them many things in parables, saying, "Behold, a sower went out to spread some seed. As he was scattering the seed, some seeds fell by the road; and the birds came and ate them up. Other seeds fell on rocky ground, where they didn't have much soil. They sprang up immediately, because the soil wasn't deep. But when the sun came up, they were scorched; and because they had no roots, they withered away. Other seeds fell among thorns, and the thorns grew and choked them out. But others fell on good soil and were producing fruit. They yielded a crop - some a hundredfold, some sixty, some thirty. He who has ears, let him hear.

Then the disciples came to Him and said, "Why do You speak to them in parables?"

And He replied to them, "To you has been given to know the secrets of the kingdom of heaven, but to them it has not been given. For whoever has, to him more will be given and he will have plenty. But whoever does not have, even what he has will be taken away from him. For this reason I speak to them in parables,

because seeing they do not see, and hearing they do not hear nor do they understand.

And in them the prophecy of Isaiah is being fulfilled, which says,

'You will keep on hearing but will never understand; you will keep on looking, but will never see.

For the heart of this people has become dull, their ears can barely hear, and they have shut their eyes.

Otherwise they might see with their eyes, and hear with their ears, and understand with their hearts. Then they would turn back, and I would heal them.'

But blessed are your eyes because they see, and your ears because they hear. Amen, I tell you, many a prophet and tzaddik longed to see what you are seeing and did not see, and to hear what you are hearing and did not hear."

"You then, hear the parable of the sower. When anyone hears the word of the kingdom and doesn't understand it, the evil one comes and snatches away what was sown in his heart. This is the one having been sown along the road.

"The one sown on rocky ground, this is the one who hears the word and immediately receives it with joy. Yet he has no root himself but lasts only a short while; and when trouble or persecution comes because of the word, immediately he falls away.

"But the one sown among the thorns, this is the one who hears the word; and the worries of the world and the seduction of wealth choke the word, and it becomes unfruitful.

"Now the one sown on the good soil, this is the one who hears the word and understands. He indeed bears fruit, and yeilding a hundredfold, some sixty, some thirty times what was sown."

The ground is the sanctuary for the seed. It is the safe place in which it can take root and grow. If the soil is too shallow, no seed can grow deep. The height that the plant or tree can soar is directly proportionate to the depth in which it is planted and the condition of the ground. It is the same with our hearts, the soil in which the seeds of G-D's Word grows. If our hearts are hard and filled with the rocks of bitterness and unforgiveness, we cannot grow to our optimal spiritual height. King David said it best in Psalm 119:11, *"I have hidden Your word in my heart that I might not sin against You."*

Look also at Mark 4:26-29:

> *And He was saying, "The kingdom of G-D is like when a man spreads seed on the soil and falls asleep at night and gets up by day, and the seed sprouts and grows. He himself doesn't know how. Automatically, the earth brings forth a crop—first the blade, then the head, then the full grain in the head. But when the grain is ready, at once he sends in the sickle, for the harvest has come."*

The ground is essential to the growth of the tree. And so it is for the believer's life and the congregation. If we are willing, we will grow where G-D plants us. Where He plants us is where He prepares the soil. When a tree grows in its home location and draws upon the environment the Lord provides, it will thrive and bear fruit in its season. If a tree is transplanted, the ground must be prepared in order to receive that tree. There is an extended time for the transplanted tree to adapt to the new surroundings and to draw upon different nutrients and soil conditions. There may be a period of shock and the possibility that the tree cannot adapt and will die.

In the natural, we tend to move from place to place without consideration for the impact. The same considerations for the transplanted tree apply to us. How much more preparation do we have to do when we leave a congregation—when we don't try to grow where G-D plants us, but leave? When we assess how much time and care it takes to prepare a place for transplanting and to make sure the new location is going to sustain the transplant, we might just find out that it would take less work to grow where we are and endure whatever trials we are going through. The Word of G-D says in Jeremiah 12:2, *"You have planted them, and they have taken root; they grow and bear fruit."* If He is the One who planted you, then shouldn't you grow and bear fruit where He plants you?

SEVEN LESSONS LEARNED FROM THE GROUND

1. Preparation *(kavannah)* is essential, and it is the preparation of the heart. If the ground is hard and rocky, nothing will grow. Likewise, if the terrain of our hearts is hard and rocky, we cannot grow. Like clay that is already hardened and cannot be reshaped, a heart that is hardened cannot be molded unless it is softened. A recipe for our spiritual growth begins with forgiveness mixed with prayer. *Kavannah* is simply the beginning of the process of preparing the heart for new seed.

2. It takes hard work to break up the soil, and we must be willing to do hard work. Faith without works is death. Psalm 128:2 says, *"You will eat the fruit of your labor; blessings and prosperity will be yours."* Hard work brings its own reward. Breaking up the hard places only has to be done once if it is done right and brings a lifetime of harvest.

3. The ground must be watered. Dry ground cannot sustain life; and unless we flow in the spirit, we cannot sustain our spiritual life. Jeremiah 2:13 states that the G-D of Israel is the spring of living water. In John 7:38, Yeshua declared, *""Whoever*

believes in Me, as the Scripture says, 'out of his inner-most being will flow rivers of living water.' We must be watered in the Word so that the ground of our hearts does not dry out.

4. We cannot break up hard ground unless we have the right tools. In the natural, the pick, the plow, and the shovel are the tools used to break up the hard ground. In the supernatural, prayer, fasting, and G-D's Word equip and prepare us.

5. From dust of the earth we are made. Let us not let pride become a stumbling block and think too highly of ourselves. We were all made from dirt. Philippians 2:3-4 says:

   Do nothing out of selfishness or conceit, but with humility consider others as more important than yourselves, looking out not only for your own interests but also for the interests of others.

6. Proverbs 28:19 says, *"He who works his land will have abundant food, but the one who chases fantasies will have his fill of poverty."* A garden worth having is a garden worth weeding—so we too must work our hearts to keep them free from evil thoughts and evil inclinations. *"We are tearing down false arguments and every high-minded thing that exalts itself against the knowledge of G-D. We are taking every thought captive to the obedience of Messiah"* (2 Cor. 10:5).

7. Psalm 80:7-9:

   Restore us, O G-D Almighty; make Your face shine upon us, that we may be saved. You brought a vine out of Egypt; You drove out the nations and planted it. You cleared the ground for it, and it took root and filled the land." The ground must be cleared.

Our hearts must be uncluttered with the worries and fears of this life so the good news of Messiah Yeshua can fill the land.

PLOWING

In Luke 6:43-49, Yeshua said:

"For there is no good tree that produces rotten fruit, nor again does a rotten tree produce good fruit. Each tree comes to be known by its own fruit. For figs are not gleaned out of briars; neither are bunches of grapes gathered from thorn bushes.

"Out of the good treasure of his heart the good mans brings forth good, and out of the evil the evil man brings forth evil. For from the overflow of the heart his mouth speaks."

"Why do you call Me 'Master, Master' and do not do what I say? Everyone who comes to Me and hears My words and does them, I will show you what he is like. He is like a man building a house, who dug deep and laid a foundation on the rock. And when a flood came, the torrent burst against that house but could not shake it, because it had been well built.

"But the one who hears yet does not do is like a man who built a house upon land without foundation. When the torrent burst against it, immediately it collapsed - and the destruction of that house was great!"

The ground must be prepared, and we must plant deep. Building on rock is wisdom and yields a great harvest. Planting on ground without a foundation may work for a season, but will not endure hardship, drought, and storms. Today, break up that hard ground and prepare a fresh, new place for the Word of G-D to take hold. Break through that old, compacted soil that has kept seed from taking hold. Shatter old thinking that keeps the roots of your faith from going deeper.

Prepare the ground of your heart to receive. Pray this personal prayer of repentance: "Lord, I am sorry I have sinned against You, and I ask Yeshua into my heart. I believe He died for my sins and He rose from the dead on the third day and is sitting at Your right hand interceding for me. Because He lives, I can live today and forevermore. In Yeshua's name. Amen."

GROUND BREAKING

With each of the seven lessons learned from the ground in Chapter 1, consider the following seven points. Take this time of introspection to plow deep, past the topsoil of your heart. Today, our journey into the tree of this life begins. We begin with the heart: the ground and the substance that makes you, you. As you continue reading, take time to ponder, make notes, and list goals as we move forward into *Lessons Learned From the Tree.*

1. *Kavannah* is a Hebrew word and implies the intentional preparation of the heart. *Kavannah* is most powerful when applied to prayer and to worship. It is only when your heart is fully prepared that you can intentionally pray and intentionally worship the Holy One of Israel. G-D has intentionally prepared *(kavannah)* the ground of your heart. All that has happened to you and all that you have been through have brought you to where you are now and to the knowledge of Messiah Yeshua. Would

you change the events of your past if you knew that changing even one thing may not lead you to the path to receiving Yeshua as Lord over your life? Stop now and forgive those who have harmed you in any way. Release them into the hands of a loving G-D. Next, break any soulish ties or negative emotions you hold against them. Now, ask *HaShem* (the Lord G-D) to bless them with shalom, healing, and if necessary, salvation. Make a list below of those you wish to release, repent to, and bless before moving further into this text.

_____

_____

_____

2. Well, you did it! You made it to step two. Congratulations! You may know by now that this walk of faith is not easy. It takes hard work to break up the soil of our hearts. What is your daily routine for forgiveness? Do you search your heart daily for bitterness and for anger? Tonight, before you fall asleep, take a few minutes and review the events of the day. Recall what you said, how you reacted, and what you did for or to another. Repent for each instance where you fell short. Let this night be the beginning of a new routine to daily "break up" the soil of your heart.

_____

_____

_____

3. The ground of your heart must be watered as dry ground cannot sustain life. Before all else, we are spirit, made *tzelem Elohim,* in the image of G-D. As spirit, we must eat spiritual food. This food waters the dry ground of our heart, sustains and nourishes our bodies and our souls. Find a daily Bible

reading plan and begin a regimen of staying in the Word regularly. Meditation on the Word of G-D is just as valuable for drenching the soul of your heart. Soak in Scripture-based music as part of your daily routine. What are other ways to saturate the ground of your heart?

_____

_____

_____

4. The right tool is important for any job. Prayer and repentance are essential tools in the walk of any believer and in the preparation of the soil of your heart. Consider adding journaling to your arsenal of tools. Journaling can uncover patterns or habits that may need to be broken. What tools are you using that benefit the *kavannah* (preparation) of your heart? What tools should you be using?

_____

_____

_____

5. Remain humble. Remember we were made to serve the Living G-D. We are servants and even bondslaves to Messiah Yeshua (see 1 Cor. 7:22). We were made for His good pleasure and to worship Him. We were made from dust, from dry ground. As you encounter others who are hard-hearted, remain humble and loving. Make a list of those who are part of your daily life and those from your extended life who, although they may have hard hearts, you desire to bless daily and to treat as you want to be treated.

_____

_____

6. Our number one goal is to live in eternity with G-D, our Creator. Every other goal in our lifetime is to line up under this one. This is truly G-D's perfect order: to put Him first. As you set long-term and short-term goals, keep eternity in the topsoil of your mind. Ask yourself, do my goals and aspirations lead me and others to eternity? *"But seek first the kingdom of G-D and His righteousness, and all these things shall be added to you"* (Matt. 6:33).

7. In a cluttered room, it is difficult to move, perform, and live. Likewise, clutter in your heart causes difficult or negative emotions, eruptions, and outbursts. The Bible tells us that out of the abundance of the heart the mouth speaks (see Matt. 12:34). Today, watch and list phrases and words you commonly speak. Do these words and phrases edify others, yourself, or G-D? Today, search for and remove clutter in your heart: unforgiveness, bitterness, and anger. What other blockages are buried in the ground of your heart? Can you release them and allow this heart-soil to be cultivated by the Holy One of Israel?

ENDNOTE

1. Dr. Donald H. Marks, MD, PhD; University of California, Los Angeles, Department of Microbiology, Immunology, and Medical Genetics.

THE SEEDS

Chapter 2

THE SEEDS

FROM MY EARLIEST RECOLLECTIONS, I can remember seeing small envelopes on our kitchen counter coated in vivid pictures of flowers and vegetables. These glossy little packets contained the smallest specks of life, and I had little understanding of the power contained within. As a child, I would walk out into the garden with my father and watch as he carefully made small rows and mounds and dropped these little flecks into the soft soil. He would then cover them, take the empty seed packet, and place it on a stick marking the end of the row. For many days, he would come home from work, change his clothes, and walk out to check for any changes in the garden.

As much as he explained to me about what would happen to the little bits he carefully placed into the manicured ground, it wasn't until I actually saw the sprouts shooting out of the soil that I began to grasp that life began in a seed. Even the tiniest seed grew into a beautiful flower or vegetable that brought value and meaning to the life that was always hidden within its hull. G-D had already programmed into it a path that, under the right conditions, would fulfill its purpose.

In the world of horticulture and agriculture, the growing of seeds is called germination. Germination is the growth of an embryonic plant contained within a seed; it results in the formation of the seedling. Seeds require soil, sunlight, and water to germinate and then literally grow on their own. Soil, sunlight, and water: how interesting that this relationship between three complex elements working in complete unity can impact life so profoundly in the natural. We see this in the supernatural as well in our relationship with the Father, Son, and Holy Spirit. It is the combination of these spiritual elements working as *one* on our hearts to break up the hard places in preparation for the seed to germinate. That seed, like us, must die to itself in order to release the plant and the fruit of the plant that lies within and activate the process that inevitably leads to the harvest. In John 12:24, Yeshua said, *"Amen, amen I tell you, unless a grain of wheat falls to the earth and dies, it remains alone. But if it dies, it produces much fruit."*

Once a seed is planted, there is a radical root that extends down into the soil with the sole purpose to seek out nutrition. From this runner, young roots grow. A stem develops and pushes its way upward out of the soil, and this becomes the stalk of the plant. Leaves grow from the stalk, and then the plant slowly takes shape. Seeds are used for propagating more plants. This purpose is clearly conveyed in the words, "be fruitful and multiply."

The seed is typically found in the flower of the plant, which has both female and male parts. When G-D created man, He created them both male and female. The male part of the flower is the stamen, which has filaments and an anther. The pollen from the anther is transferred to the pistil and the female part, called the ovary. And this is how germination takes place. When the conditions are suitable, then the seeds steadily grow, reaching the stage of pollination.

Pollination is carried out in the flowers by insects like bees, butterflies, and moths, and also by tiny birds, which come hungrily looking for nectar. Even in the seed, even in the flower, even in the simple example that G-D gives us with the fundamentals of the tree, we see G-D's creative hand. In the same way life begins and bursts forth in humans, it begins and bursts forth in the plant life.

On June 12, 2005, the following story appeared in Israel:

> In Jerusalem, a date palm seedling, planted on January 25, has grown up to stand 14 inches high; it has five leaves and is nicknamed Methuselah. While it may look like any other ordinary palm seedling, for Dr. Elaine Solowey, UCLA-educated botanist, it is a piece of history brought back to life. Growing in the black pot in Solowey's nursery is a seed 2,000 years old, more than twice as old as the 969-year-old biblical character who lent his name to the young tree. It is the oldest seed ever known to produce a viable young tree. The seed that produced "Methuselah" was discovered during archeological excavations of King Herod's palace on Mt. Masada near the Dead Sea. Its age has been confirmed by modern science as a 2,000-year-old seed producing life.[1]

In the lineage and history of the Bible, *seed* is also translated as "offspring." This fascinating story of the Methuselah seed gives us insight into how a seed can remain dormant until the optimal conditions exist for its germination. All seeds house a dormant, fertilized plant embryo. Most feature a hard outer shell that protects the embryo from premature germination, extreme weather, and predators. Seeds lie dormant beneath the soil until they receive the proper amount of warmth, sunlight, and moisture, at which time they germinate. These are the catalysts that act upon the seed to initiate its life cycle.

We read in Genesis 3:15, *"And I will put enmity between you and the woman, and between your offspring and hers; he will crush your head, and you will strike his heel."* Of course he's talking about Messiah crushing the head of *hasatan* (satan). This passage alone had a profound impact on me as I read the Hebrew Scriptures. I recall many times looking for the event where the seed of the woman crushed the head of the seed of the serpent. In my search through the Tanakh, I could never find where this event took place, and I questioned how there could be unfinished business if all that was written in the Bible was true.

As I studied the life cycle of the seed and the catalysts that act upon it to bring it forth, I began to see a profound connection between the passages in Genesis 3:15 and Luke 1:26-37:

> *Then in the sixth month, the angel Gabriel was sent by ADONAI into a town in the Galilee named Natzeret, and to a virgin engaged to a man named Joseph, of the house of David. The virgin's name was Miriam. And coming to her, the angel said, "Shalom, favored one! ADONAI is with you." But at the message, she was perplexed and kept wondering what kind of greeting this might be. The angel spoke to her, "Do not be afraid, Miriam, for you have found favor with G-D. Behold, you will become pregnant and give birth to a son, and you shall call His name Yeshua. He will be great and will be called Ben-Elyon. ADONAI Elohim will give Him the throne of David, His father. He shall reign over the house of Jacob for all eternity, and His kingdom will be without end."*

Miriam said to the angel, "How can this be, since I am not intimate with a man?"

And responding, the angel said to her, 'The Ruach ha-Kodesh will come upon you, and the power of Elyon will overshadow you. Therefore, the Holy One being born will be called Ben-Elohim."

After reading the story of the Methuselah seed and understanding the dormancy of seeds, I had new insight into what occurred in the natural to bring about a supernatural event. The seed of the woman that lay dormant throughout the generations was now activated and germinated by the *Ruach HaKodesh*, the Holy Spirit of G-D.

In Genesis 13:14-15, the Lord said to Abram:

Lift up your eyes from where you are and look north and south, east and west. All the land that you see I will give to you and your offspring forever. I will make your offspring like the dust of the earth, so that if anyone could count the dust, then your offspring could be counted. Go, walk through the length and breadth of the land, for I am giving it to you.

This covenant was a land covenant and an inheritance for the Jewish people to inhabit and to prosper. In order for the people to prosper, the land had to be able to support the seed of the Jewish people through the natural planting of seed to sustain life. Mark Twain, who visited Israel in 1867, described it like this in *The Innocents Abroad*:

We traversed some miles of desolate country whose soil is rich enough but is given wholly to weeds—a silent, mournful expanse.... A desolation is here that not even imagination can grace with the pomp of life and action. We reached Tabor safely.... We never saw a human being on the whole route. We pressed on toward the goal of our crusade, renowned Jerusalem. The further we went the hotter the sun got and the more rocky and bare, repulsive and dreary the landscape became.... There was hardly a tree or a shrub anywhere. Even the olive and the cactus, those fast friends of a worthless soil, had almost deserted the country. No landscape exists that is more tiresome to the eye than that which bounds the approaches to Jerusalem.... Jerusalem is mournful, dreary and lifeless. I would not desire to live here. It is a hopeless, dreary, heartbroken land....[2]

In 1882, 15 years after Mark Twain's visit, some 30,000 Jews immigrated to Israel; they came in two waves between 1882 and 1891 and founded 28 new settlements. Hundreds of thousands of acres were purchased by these early Zionists from absentee Arab landowners who usually lived elsewhere in the Middle East. The majority of the lands purchased were in areas that were neglected and considered undevelopable—such as the sandy coastal plain or the swampy, malaria-infested Hula Valley in the north. Amazingly, and with much effort, these early settlers made the barren land bloom again and drained the swamps.

G-D's instruction is clear, both in the natural and in the spiritual, for He says in Deuteronomy 22:9, *"Do not plant two kinds of seed in your vineyard; if you do, not only the crops you plant but also the fruit of the vineyard will be defiled."* Certainly there is a well-defined picture here in the natural, and we can imagine how two crops could become entangled and defiled.

In the spiritual realm, we can equate the two seeds to faith and fear. Faith and fear combined are mingled seeds in opposition to each other. Fear defiles faith! As we apply the instructions of Deuteronomy 22:9 to our lives, we can hear clearly, *"Do not plant both faith and fear in your life; otherwise, your harvest will be defiled."* A field planted with mingled seed would be in the same condition as a double-minded person who is unstable in all he or she does.

In Ecclesiastes 3:1-8, we read:

> *There is a time for everything, and a season for every activity under heaven: a time to be born and a time to die, a time to plant and a time to uproot, a time to kill and a time to heal, a time to tear down and a time to build, a time to weep and a time to laugh, a time to mourn and a time to dance, a time to scatter stones and a time to gather them, a time to embrace and a time to refrain, a time to search and a time to give up, a time to keep and a time to throw away, a time to tear and a time to mend, a time to be silent and a time to speak, a time to love and a time to hate, a time for war and a time for peace.*

No one plants when the ground is frozen, for the time and the season are not right for planting. Even for us as a people, timing is everything. The seed that we sow as believers in Messiah Yeshua is not a physical plant seed, but it is the Word of G-D. As we take the Word and go out into the community to sow seeds, we must be sure that we first understand the condition of the soil and prepare the soil of another's heart before we deposit the seed. Our approach must be one of love as we make ready that soil and as we sow seeds into that undeveloped soil of the heart. We do that in the same way that farmers study the soil composition. They examine what condition the soil is in before they start to add ingredients. It is not beneficial to overfertilize or overwater. Understanding the soil's condition determines not only the right time to plant, but also which seed will benefit from the soil's condition. Ecclesiastes 11:6 says, *"Sow your seed in the morning, and at evening let not your hands be idle, for you do not know which will succeed, whether this or that, or whether both will do equally well."*

We must also prepare the soil to plant the right seed at the right time in the properly prepared place:

> *Listen and hear My voice; pay attention and hear what I say. When a farmer plows for planting, does he plow continually? Does he keep on breaking up and harrowing the soil? When he has leveled the surface, does he not sow caraway and scatter cumin? Does he not plant wheat in its place, barley in its plot, and spelt in its field? His G-D instructs him and teaches him the right way"* (Isaiah 28:23-26).

So not only is timing everything, but each seed has a place within the garden. Each place within the field is prepared for each seed, and we don't continue to plow past the point of readiness.

In Matthew 13:24-30, we read:

> *He presented to them another parable, saying, "The kingdom of heaven is like a man who sowed good seed in his field. But while the men were sleeping, his enemy came and sowed weeds among the wheat and went away. Now when the stalk sprouted and produced grain, then the weeds also appeared. So the slaves of the landowner came and said to him, 'Master, didn't you sow good seed in your field? Then where did the weeds come from?' But he replied, 'An enemy did this.' Now the slaves say to him,*

'Do you want us, then, to go out and gather them up?' But he says, 'No, for while you are gathering up the weeds, you may uproot the wheat with them. Let both grow together until the harvest. At harvest time, I will tell the reapers, 'First, gather up the weeds and tie them in bundles to burn them up; but gather the wheat into my barn.'''

Along with discerning the soil type, we must also have discernment in the harvest. In other words, we must separate the good from the bad. In our lives, good seed has been sown into our hearts, but seeds of doubt have also been sown. Seeds have been sown into us by loving parents, by teachers that meant well, by pastors and rabbis who spoke into our lives and planted seeds in us that did not always mature. The enemy has also spoken into us, and we know that he can only speak lies. Like the farmer in the parable, we must wait for the harvest so we can discern between the wheat and the weeds. We must then tie those weeds together and burn them so that our harvest is only rich and plentiful. We must examine the harvest and only hold on to what is beneficial and healthy. In nature, the heat of the fire burns off the remains to prepare a clean place for the next planting. Unless we clear out the weeds, they will creep into the next harvest, and we will be in the same condition again.

In Matthew 13:31-43, we read:

He presented to them another parable, saying, "The kingdom of heaven is like a mustard seed, which a man took and planted in his field. It's the smallest of all seeds; yet when it's full grown, it's greater than the other herbs. It becomes like a tree, so that the birds of the air come and nest in its branches."

He told them another parable, "The kingdom of heaven is like hametz, which a woman took and hid in three measures of flour, until it was all leavened."

All these things Yeshua spoke to the crowds in parables. And apart from a parable, He wasn't speaking to them, in order to fulfill what was spoken through the prophet, saying, "I will open My mouth in parables, I will utter things hidden since the foundation of the world."

Then He sent the crowds away and went into the house. His disciples came to Him, saying, "Explain to us the parable of the weeds of the field."

He answered, "The one sowing the good seed is the Son of Man, and the field is the world. And the good seed, these are the sons of the kingdom; and the weeds are the sons of the evil one. The enemy who sowed them is the devil, the harvest is the end of the age, and the reapers are angels. Therefore just as the weeds are gathered up and burned with fire, so shall it be at the end of the age. The Son of Man will send forth His angels, and they will gather out of His kingdom all stumbling blocks and those who practice lawlessness. They will throw them into the fiery furnace; in that place will be weeping and gnashing of teeth. Then the righteous will shine forth as the sun in the kingdom of their Father. He who has ears, let him hear!"

SEVEN LESSONS LEARNED FROM THE SEEDS

1. Seeds are small, and when planted in the right conditions, their potential is great. From among the smallest of seeds, the mustard seed, grows the largest of trees. *"Then the Lord said, 'If you have*

faith like a mustard seed, you could say to this mulberry tree, "Be uprooted and planted in the sea,' and it would obey you"' (Luke 17:6). You may think your faith is small, but once applied, even a little faith can grow into something big.

2. Seeds send down a runner beneath the surface. Before making an appearance above ground, the seed first grows beneath the surface. In the same way, we must first go deep in order to find the source of living water to sustain our lives. We must go deep into the Word of G-D lest we build ourselves on a foundation of shifting sand and get blown over in the first storm that comes into our lives. We must first grow beneath the surface.

3. A seed can remain dormant like the Methuselah plant that grew after 2,000 years. So we must exhibit patience and wait on G-D's timing to grow. Keep on planting and walking by faith, believing that what we've sown into our lives and our children's lives will grow into a bountiful harvest.

4. Seeds require the right conditions—soil, sunlight, and water—just as our growth requires the whole package, the Father, the Son, and the *Ruach HaKodesh,* the Holy Spirit. Remove one of the elements and the seed does not germinate and grow. They must work in unity to produce the healthiest crop both in the natural and in the supernatural. Too much water, too much light, or too much heat can kill the plant. We too must keep a life in balance so that we maintain the mind of

Messiah in all things. It is the spiritual mind that equips us for daily life and allows us to maintain balance.

5. What you sow is what you get. *"Then G-D said, 'Let the land produce vegetation: seed-bearing plants and trees on the land that bear fruit with seed in it, according to their various kinds.' And it was so. The land produced vegetation: plants bearing seed according to their kinds and trees bearing fruit with seed in it according to their kinds"* (Gen. 1:11-12). We cannot plant apple seeds and be disappointed when we do not get cucumbers. Seeds of doubt yield a harvest too, and what we sow we will reap.

6. We did not create the seed, yet we reap the harvest. We are guardians of the seed and are charged with planting it in fertile soil to reap a harvest for the Kingdom of G-D. Let us share the seed with others so they may also enjoy and be well-fed.

7. There's a time to plant. Timing is everything. When we plant, we are to take the time to prepare the soil so that the best environment exists for the success of the seed. Planting too early is just as bad as planting too late. As we plant the seed of the Word in others, let us be sensitive to the right time to plant and the right time to harvest.

SOWING NEW SEEDS

What seeds have you been planting in your life? Is today the day for you to harvest what has been sown in you? Is today the day that the seed of the Lord takes hold in your life and brings a harvest—a harvest that brings new life and provision where there's been no provision? Is this the day He brings a harvest that will transform your fields from barren and filled with weeds to prosperous and overflowing? You ask, "How do I get that kind of field?"

You say "yes" to the One who came for you. You say "yes" to the One about whom G-D spoke to the woman when He said, "Your seed will crush the head of the serpent" (see Gen. 3:15). He was speaking of Messiah Yeshua. If you want a new harvest in your life, you have to plant new seed. If you want things to change, you have to make changes in your life, your thoughts, and your way of doing things. You have to do things different from how you have ever done them before. Say, "Yes, I want a new harvest in my life. I want to plant new seeds. I want to turn this old field under. I want to claim for my life Second Corinthians 5:17, *'Therefore if anyone is in Messiah, he is a new creation. The old things have passed away; behold, all things have become new.'*" If you want a new season in your life say "yes" to Yeshua. How do you say yes? You say, "Lord, I am sorry I sinned against You, and I ask Yeshua into my heart. I believe He died for me and rose on the third day and is sitting at the right hand of G-D interceding for me. Because He lives, I can live now and forevermore. Amen."

SOWING GOOD SEEDS

1. Scatter seeds by handing out compliments (deserved and otherwise), greeting others with smiles, and helping and serving all people. Then pray for all those dispersed seeds. In this way, you will water those seeds. Practice this type of seed sowing every day, and soon you will enjoy a bumper crop of harvest.

As you check on those newly planted seeds, remember to also add water by praying G-D's will and His Word over all those lives you touch. Write a short prayer in the space below for those people who received seeds from you today. Perhaps you have started thinking about or even begun planting good seeds into the lives of those you love. That's pretty easy, isn't it? Now, consider someone unlovely, and as Romans 12:21 says, *"Do not be overcome by evil, but overcome evil with good."* Bless them with good seeds in the way you would with those you love. That, favored one, is unconditional love.

_____

_____

2. Create a prayer journal and add to it those in whom you are planting good seeds. From this chapter, we learn that seeds send down a runner beneath the surface in order to discover water. Sometimes you will be the "tap root" in another's life. You'll do that by praying without ceasing. First Samuel 12:23 says, *"As for me, far be it from me that I should sin against the Lord by failing to pray for you."* Diligently, fervently even, pray for those seeds you have planted in others. Pray. Wait. Pray some more. Wait some more. The seed will make its appearance if the ground is well-watered, well-nourished, and has *Son*light. Never give up on anyone. G-D never gave up on you.

_____

_____

_____

3. What if the seeds you planted in the hearts of those you love and those you have a harder time loving never sprout or reach the surface to be seen by others? Be encouraged! G-D's Word never returns void. That's why you must utilize the Word of G-D as you pray for others. The seed may not surface or have breakthrough until the very end of its life, or not possibly until the next generation. Seeds germinate at different rates depending on many variables. Likewise, be patient with the little seed and let it have its being in G-D's will. Make a list of dormant seeds and beside each one write, *"Romans 8:28—Now we know that all things work together for good...."* Some seeds just never see the light of day. Still, be encouraged and continue seeding the hearts of those all around you.

_____

_____

_____

4. Under just the right conditions, the seed bursts forth from the ground. What are the right conditions? Wikipedia says that "right" is an ethical concept and the opposite of wrong. For you and I, there is only one ethical concept that is the opposite of wrong: Yeshua. Have you told your family member, friend, or acquaintance about Him? If you have and if you are waiting on them to make a decision, write their names down and start a new prayer list entitled: "Pre-Believers." Pray for their salvation daily. *Son*light, together with watering with the Word, provides the "right" conditions for the soil in any heart.

_____

_____

_____

5. Take a moment and recall the seeds you have planted into the lives of others. Also think about the seeds you are planning to plant. Now, check your own faith. Are you 100 percent certain and 100 percent sincere about what you have said or will say? Planting seeds of doubt into the vulnerable soil of another's heart will reap doubt. Certainly those seeds were all planted in love. Love can be the greatest nutrient given to tender seeds: *"Now the goal of this command is love from a pure heart and a clear conscience and a genuine faith"* (1 Tim. 1:5). If necessary, make a list of those in whom you have possibly planted seeds of doubt. Then pray a prayer of forgiveness, repentance, and blessing over each name. Continue this process until you see a softening of the heart in this area or until you feel a release from the Lord to stop praying.

---

6. Who had the greatest and most constructive impact in your life and why? Did they love you or show you respect? I'll bet they did. Use the example of these special people (or person) to discover the right conditions to prepare a heart for successful sowing and reaping. Write out in the space below their name(s) and what you learned and desire to pass to others. Then spread these seeds around. Actually, you already do. The seed that was planted in you is now bearing healthy fruit, and you know what is right and good and should be shared. Can you trace how many generations back this seed, habit, or process may go? G-D says there will be seedtime and harvest as long as the Earth remains (see Gen. 8:22). Plant good seeds in love into the next generation.

---

7. Ecclesiastes 3 begins, *"There is a time for everything, and a season for every activity under heaven: a time to be born and a time to die, a time to plant and a time to uproot...."* Timing is everything. When have you heard of a farmer planting during a hard freeze? You haven't—because the soil is unprepared. In your season of planting seeds, consider the soil and discern which is good for planting. Look for a teachable heart. Look for softness and love in the heart. Salvation and strong belief in Messiah Yeshua as Lord is a sign of a heart ready to receive. As for nonbelievers you encounter, aim for an appropriate seedtime when they ask you about your faith or comment on your shalom (peace), etc. Actively listen to everything that is said to you. Then discern how the Lord would have you respond. What other indicators can you think of that describe a heart which is malleable and ready for planting the good seeds you desire to share?

ENDNOTES

1. Steven Erlanger, "After 2,000 Years, a Seed from Ancient Judea Sprouts," *The New York Times,* June 12, 2005. See http://www.nytimes.com/2005/06/12/international/middleeast/12palm.html; accessed January 26, 2012.

2. Mark Twain, *The Innocents Abroad* (Oxford, UK: John Beaufoy Pub., 2009).

THE
ROOTS

Chapter 3

THE ROOTS

I REMEMBER A TIME WHEN my wife, Lora, and I served as *shamishim* (servants) on the deacon board at Congregation Beth Hallel in Roswell, Georgia, where I was spiritually raised, where I came to know the Lord, and where I was shepherded and became a disciple in the ministry. We were very blessed in our season there under the leadership of Rabbi Robert Israel Solomon.

One of the wonderful people who came into my life was a man whose Hebrew name was Baruch Ben Svi. We called him Bruce. Bruce was also one of the *shamishim,* and thus we became good friends. I was a service leader, and he was also a service leader as well as a cantor. We stood side by side ministering to the congregation many times over the years. As he cantored, I would lead services.

One of my jobs in the congregation was to schedule the leadership meetings. As a result, I received a phone call on a Monday afternoon from Rabbi Solomon saying, "Please call all the leadership together. We're going to have a meeting on Thursday. Make sure you get in touch with everybody on the board. This is an important meeting, and I need to hear back from you right away that you have personally spoken to everyone."

In compliance with the instructions given, I pulled out my directory and began calling everyone on the list. This was not a big task because I had solid contact information for all the leaders. Bruce was the only one who did not have a cell number, so I called his home number and left him a message. Like all the leadership, Bruce was prompt about getting back to me—usually the same day, but certainly no later than the next day. The next morning went by and I didn't hear from Bruce, so I called again. I was a little surprised when no one answered as I knew for sure they were not out of town. And besides, I was certain that his wife, Linda, would answer. I left Bruce another message. I didn't really know what happened to him but it was unusual that I didn't hear from him. After several failed attempts, I sent an e-mail to his home e-mail address, but I received no response. Tuesday was our regular Bible study night, and I was certain I would see Bruce there.

When Rabbi Solomon asked me for an update, I shared with him my unsuccessful efforts to reach Bruce. We agreed that this lack of communication was unusual, but we would surely see him at Bible study and there was no reason for concern. However, as the hours passed and so did the Bible study that night, Bruce never did arrive.

Soon it was Wednesday, and I was calling a couple times a day because I don't know what's going on with Bruce. I can't reach him. I can't reach his wife, Linda. There's just no answer and there's no return call. And so I called Rabbi Solomon and said, "Do you know if there's anything going on with Bruce and Linda?" He replied, "No, I've been trying to reach them. I can't get them either." This is so unusual. He's faithful, faithful, faithful; he always returns phone calls; he is at every meeting, at every service, always there, always there, always, always there. I continued to call him all day Wednesday. Wednesday night I called. I called at all hours. They had a dog at home, and I knew that the dog was old and needed care. They would never leave the dog home for hours and especially for days. I called around to friends and said, "Do you know what's happened to Bruce?" And they said, "No, we've been trying to reach him, too." I said, "It's so unusual for him to drop off the radar."

Finally, Thursday afternoon Bruce called me and said, "Listen, I'm really sorry. I've been out working in my garden." I said, "Well, Bruce, that's really no excuse for not calling me."

He goes on to tell me, "No, I was out there on Sunday; we're getting the house ready to sell, and I was trying to clean up the yard. I have these roots in my yard, and they were really giving me fits. I finally got hold of this one vine-like root. It was black, and it was about a quarter inch in diameter. I began pulling on it because if I didn't pull it out completely it was just going to sprout again and continue to take over the yard. So I grabbed this black vine-like root. I pulled on it, and it was coming up, and it seemed endless. I had to get to the root, so I followed it around the back of the house. Finally, I was so frustrated and tired I just decided to take my shovel and cut it. I've never seen anything like it. You wouldn't believe all the colors that were inside this vine—red and yellow; this root was amazing. So I called the Garden Center at Home Depot and said, 'I've cut this black vine-like root, and inside of it are all these different colors. I've never seen anything like it. What kind is it?' He said, 'Telephone.'"

That was the root of the problem! Getting to the root of the problem is good in all cases. But cutting the wrong root can have far-reaching consequences.

As we study the roots, we explore two specific functions of the root. The first function is the absorption of water and inorganic nutrients; and the second function is the anchoring of the plant body to the ground. Without any kind of root system, the plant would just blow away. From our study of the seed in Chapter 2 of this book, we know that the seed germinates. It sends down a radical root into the ground to find the water source and to anchor it so that the tree can sprout. Once it grows down, it can grow up. The root's intention is to seek out food and water, and while on this mission, it sends out branches that provide an underground infrastructure of support. The roots become the very foundation by which the tree can grow to its full significance.

There are two main threats to the survival of roots. When a plant grows too large for its container, it becomes root bound with no room for additional growth. The roots become tangled, matted, and they continue to grow in circles. Roots that travel in this circular fashion become a noose and ultimately choke the very tree they are trying to support. Root-bound plants placed in the ground without having the roots unraveled or trimmed often fail to overcome their choked conditions. This results in stunting the plants' growth and potential, and ultimately leads to their death.

The other threatening condition we know about is root rot. As indicated in the name, the roots of the plant rot. Usually, this is a result of overwatering. In house plants, it is a very common problem and slightly less common in outdoor plants. In both indoor and outdoor plants, however, it is usually lethal, and there is no treatment. The excess water makes it difficult for the roots to get the air that they need, making them rot.

We previously identified three elements that must work in perfect balance in order to sustain the life of the seed. They were soil, sunlight (as a source of heat), and water. These were the elements that stimulated and supported the metamorphosis from a seed to a germinated seed sending forth roots. Now that the seed has begun to send out its roots, it requires oxygen. Lack of oxygen reduces root respiration, which affects its ability to synthesize sunlight. If plants don't get a precise balance of air, water, and sunlight, they cannot survive. This is yet another example of the relationship between three critical elements working in perfect harmony.

The same lesson we learned in Chapter 2 is repeated here. In G-D's economy, He repeats that which is important so that we understand the significant role of all parts working together in perfect harmony. In the same way that we suffer when we do not break the unhealthy patterns in our lives, a plant with root rot will not normally survive.

As we examine the parts of the tree, we have already explored the ground that the seed is planted in and investigated the seed itself. As the seed germinates and takes root, the roots establish a complex system that send out feeder roots that in turn anchor the tree to the earth below and create a network that provides the distribution of water and nutrients to the tree itself. In the same way, G-D shows us how the spiritual and physical root, Israel, created life for the children of Israel and became the source of life for all mankind through the Messiah.

In Psalm 80:8-19, the Word of G-D says:

> *You brought a vine out of Egypt; You drove out the nations and planted it. You cleared the ground for it, and it took root and filled the land. The mountains*

71

were covered with its shade, the mighty cedars with its branches. It sent out its boughs to the Sea, its shoots as far as the River.

Why have You broken down its walls so that all who pass by pick its grapes? Boars from the forest ravage it and the creatures of the field feed on it. Return to us, O G-D Almighty! Look down from heaven and see! Watch over this vine, the root Your right hand has planted, the son You have raised up for Yourself.

Your vine is cut down, it is burned with fire; at Your rebuke Your people perish. Let Your hand rest on the man at Your right hand, the son of man You have raised up for Yourself. Then we will not turn away from You; revive us, and we will call on Your name.

Restore us, O Lord G-D Almighty; make Your face shine upon us, that we may be saved.

When we read this excerpt from Psalms, we see the perfect picture of Israel and the portrayal of Israel's salvation: Yeshua. Just as the root of the tree has two specific functions, so also the root in G-D's economy has two functions. The root by G-D's standards serves to establish the covenant relationship with His people through the physical land of Israel and the spiritual salvation of Israel and all mankind through the Messiah. Without the root from G-D going forth, planting salvation and making atonement for our sins, we would all be condemned to separation from G-D, for every inclination of our hearts are wicked: *"You are not a G-D who takes pleasure in evil; with You the wicked cannot dwell"* (Ps. 5:4).

Proverbs 12:3 tells us, *"A man cannot be established through wickedness, but the righteous cannot be uprooted."* There may be many ways to kill a tree, but the most effective is to uproot it. For the life of the tree is in the roots. Without them there is no foundation and no system of nourishment. *"The wicked desire the plunder of evil men, but the root of the righteous flourishes"* (Prov. 12:12).

There are many stories of immigrants from the Mediterranean Region wrapping the roots of age-old vines in cloth to bring to America for planting. These vines, like their ancestors, were either from cuttings or from the roots of other vines that were transplanted. Wherever they were planted, they adapted and cross-pollinated with the local varieties to bring a unique flavor to their fruit.

In this chapter on the roots, we again see G-D using the things of the natural to reveal supernatural insights to us. As G-D dispersed His people to the four corners of the world, we see how we have been transplanted and that He has reserved for Himself a remnant from the root and will raise up a Savior from this root:

> *In that day the Root of Jesse will stand as a banner for the peoples; the nations will rally to Him, and His place of rest will be glorious* (Isa. 11:10).

> *Who has believed our message and to whom has the arm of the Lord been revealed? He grew up before Him like a tender shoot, and like a root out of dry ground. He had no beauty or majesty to attract us to Him...* (Isa. 53:1-2).

The prophet Isaiah goes on to tell us there was nothing in His appearance that we should desire Him. As in the parable the Lord gave me, when the beautiful leaves fall off the tree, we just pass it by, yet the root goes deeper and no one sees. Nothing in its appearance is beautiful to us anymore. If it's not glorious and beautiful like the robe of Joseph or like the garments of Solomon, we lose interest. Yet in this parable G-D shows us Messiah, and He tells us, like a root out of dry ground, He had no beauty or majesty to attract us to Him. He shows us that there was nothing in His appearance that we should desire Him. But from the root will burst forth life in the natural and in the supernatural.

> This is what the Lord says: "Cursed is the one who trusts in man, who depends on flesh for his strength and whose heart turns away from the Lord. He will be like a bush in the wastelands; he will not see prosperity when it comes. He will dwell on the parched places of the desert, in a salt land where no one lives. But blessed is the man who trusts in the Lord, whose confidence is in Him. He will be like a tree planted by the water that sends out its roots by the stream. It does not fear when heat comes; its leaves are always green. It has no worries in a year of drought and never fails to bear fruit" (Jer. 17:5-8).

In Hebrews 12:15, G-D cautions us about root rot: "See to it that no one falls short of the grace of G-D; and see to it that no bitter root springs up and causes trouble, and by it many be defiled." The ground is our heart, and the seed is the Word, and the root is Messiah. G-D calls Him a root, and out of dry ground He brings forth a root that will give life to Israel and all mankind. As we examine the Tree of Life, we see that the *Etz*, the Word of G-D, is that Tree of Life that contains the very key to eternal life: and the Word was G-D. And as we explore the Word of G-D and the passages Yeshua quoted, we return to the Torah. It was from the Torah that Yeshua taught, and it is no coincidence that the Torah is mounted on *Etz Chaim* and is itself referred to as a Tree of Life.

In Matthew 5:17-19, Yeshua Himself said:

> *Do not think that I came to abolish the Torah or the Prophets! I did not come to abolish, but to fulfill. Amen, I tell you, until heaven and earth pass away, not the smallest letter or serif shall ever pass away from the Torah until all things come to pass. Therefore, whoever breaks one of the least of these commandments, and teaches others the same, shall be called least in the kingdom of heaven. But whoever keeps and teaches them, this one shall be called great in the kingdom of heaven.*

As believers in Yeshua, we uphold the Torah, the instruction that all the Word of G-D contains. It is by choice and not under compulsion we embrace the wisdom of the Word of G-D. It is by choice and not under compulsion we herald the Word of G-D. It is by choice and not under compulsion we study the Word of G-D. The Word of G-D says to study to show yourself approved (see 2 Tim. 2:15). Romans chapter 2 clearly shows that a Jewish person who embraces the Torah is doing what is expected, but a non-Jewish person who embraces the Torah is called righteous.

In G-D's economy, what He shows us in the natural is a shadow of what is in the supernatural. The root of the tree has two purposes: for the absorption of water and as an anchor. In the supernatural, the root is Messiah and Israel. If we are to go deep, we must allow Messiah to take hold of our lives, and He must be our anchor. Our hearts must be turned to Israel for the restoration of His covenant land and His covenant people so that Messiah will return. Remember Messiah's words in Matthew 23:37-39:

> *O Jerusalem, Jerusalem who kills the prophets and stones those sent to her! How often I longed to gather your children together, as a hen gathers her chicks under her wings, but you were not willing! Look, your house is left to you desolate! For I tell you, you will never see Me again until you say, "Baruch ha-ba b'shem ADONAI. Blessed is He who comes in the name of the Lord!"*

G-D has entrusted us with His Word to embrace it as a Tree of Life—to take hold of it and go out and make disciples. We cannot harvest if we do not plant. We cannot plant if we do not plow. The seed cannot germinate and take root if it does not have the right conditions.

SEVEN LESSONS LEARNED FROM THE ROOTS

1. Like the seed, roots grow beneath the surface. It's not about the outward appearance but about what grows beneath our surface. Man looks on the outward appearance; G-D looks on the heart. We must not only go beneath the surface in order to establish a firm foundation, but we must go deep into the Word for nourishment and living water to sustain us in desert situations.

2. The root has the power to break through hard ground, and we must be willing to persevere, to break through the hard ground so that we would take root in the Word and be of service in the Body of Messiah. Romans 5:1-5 says:

Therefore, having been made righteous by trusting, we have shalom with G-D through our Lord Yeshua the Messiah. Through Him we also have gained access by faith into this grace in which we stand and boast in the hope of G-D's glory. And not only that, but we also boast in suffering—knowing that suffering produces perseverance; and perseverance, character; and character, hope. And hope does not disappoint, because G-D's love has been poured into our hearts through the Ruach ha-Kodesh who was given us.

3. The root takes the path that goes around obstacles. When the root comes to a rock, it finds a way to continue on its path. It just doesn't hit the rock and stop. It will press on until it goes over, under, around, or through the obstacle in its path. We are also called to the same path as the root.

   Not that I have already obtained this or been perfected, but I press on if only I might take hold of that for which Messiah Yeshua took hold of me. Brothers and sisters, I do not consider myself as having taken hold of this. But this one thing I do: forgetting what is behind and straining toward what is ahead, I press on toward the goal for the reward of the upward calling of G-D in Messiah Yeshua (Phil. 3:12-14).

4. The root seeks out water; we too, as believers, must seek out living water. We must seek out the Word of G-D. We must seek out relationship with

the Holy Spirit, for He is our living water. Just as the tree planted by the water does not fear or worry because its life source is secure, we are to also walk without fear or worry because He who is in us is greater than he who is in the world (see 1 John 4:4). We cannot live by faith if we are not drawing on the river of life and the Source of living water, Messiah Yeshua.

5. The root becomes an anchor for support. The tree does not support the root; the root supports the tree. We don't support the root; the root supports us. And for us who are the grafted-in natural or wild branches, we are reminded by Rabbi Shaul (Paul) that we don't support the root; the root supports us (see Rom. 11:17-21). Let us not think so highly of ourselves that we believe that we've come to replace G-D's plan for Israel and for His people. We've come to be part of it as co-inheritors and co-laborers in this vineyard. We should work together so that we reap the riches and great reward that G-D has for us as we labor together for the harvest—our people's salvation. G-D's plan is for Jew and Gentile to become one in Messiah. How can you have one new man if you don't have two old men? Let us walk humbly in the role G-D has given us, not trying to be what we are not. It is through our differences, our joining together in unity, that salvation will be brought about.

6. It is the complex root system that goes deepest. As we grow, we are to go deeper in G-D's Word. If we're not growing, we're dying. If the tree is not growing, it's dying. We can no longer lean on our own understanding or take the word of others as to what G-D is saying. We are responsible for our own growth in the Lord. No one wants to be dependent on others for physical nourishment, so why do we allow ourselves to become dependent on others for our spiritual nourishment? We must go deeper to find truths hidden deep in the Word of G-D.

7. There's a direct correlation to the depth, breadth, and height a tree can soar based on how deep, how complex, and how long its root is. It is what's beneath the surface that determines how high, how broad, how large, and how powerful a tree can become. It is the same with our lives. G-D does not call the qualified; He qualifies the called. We must be faithful in our daily Bible reading and our daily prayer life in order to be equipped for the day of our calling. If we have a desire to be used by G-D, we must go deep and be firmly established in His Word so that we can grow to the heights that He desires for us.

BENEATH THE SURFACE

If your heart is thirsty and if your spirit is dry, come and drink. Let your roots go down to the living water:

"I, Yeshua, have sent My angel to testify these things to you for My communities.

I am the Root and the Offspring of David, the Bright and Morning Star." The Ruach and the bride say, "Come!"

And let the one who hears say, "Come!" Let the one who is thirsty come—let the one who wishes freely take the water of life! (Rev. 22:16-17)

In John 4:13-14, Yeshua said to the woman at the well:

Everyone who drinks from this water will get thirsty again. But whoever drinks of the water that I will give him shall never be thirsty. The water that I give him will become a fountain of water within him, springing up to eternal life!

Yeshua is the root to the Tree of Life. He came to bring new life, to send us down deep into the Word to seek out living water. As we study these lessons learned from the tree, we see that in G-D's economy we must go deeper. We must plant ourselves to reach for the water, to be anchored so when the storms of our life come by, we are not blown over and uprooted. Instead, we're planted firmly in the Word of G-D so that our faith will be unshaken.

Yeshua grew up like a tender shoot. He was not beautiful. There was nothing about His outward appearance that would attract men to Him. This is your time. This is the time of His coming into your life. Allow these living waters to flow first into your life, and then back into the world. The seeds that have been planted by G-D's Word are taking hold in your hearts. Where there has been dry ground, let the water of His Spirit flow forth. You may be saying, "I'm dry, and I'm thirsty. I'm in a dry place, and I need a drink. I'm root bound. I've got root rot. I've got bitterness growing in my heart. I need a release."

Yeshua walked this Earth not to bring peace but to bring a sword, a sword that would separate us from a life of sin, hunger, thirst, and loneliness. The Word of G-D is a sword, and if you don't have the sword in your life, you don't have that drink from that living water. If your roots are not going deep because you don't have a personal relationship with Yeshua, I give you the opportunity to say this simple prayer: "Lord, I'm sorry. I'm sorry that I've sinned against You."

In the Book of Isaiah, the Jewish prophet Isaiah says, "Your sins were once as red as scarlet, but now they're as white as snow" (see Isa. 1:18). And for you who have never said "yes" to Yeshua, the promised Jewish Messiah, your sins are as red as scarlet—but they can be made as white as snow.

GROWING DEEPER

1. "In G-D's economy" is a phrase that forces us to take a different, otherworldly perspective. This perspective is radical, unchanging, and in most cases unimagined. In G-D's economy, beauty takes place beneath the surface. It is an outward response to an inward appearance. Beauty is the result of something molded by G-D below the surface. Consider your words. Before they are spoken, they are born in your heart and your mind. The mouth is opened, and it overflows...with what? Bitterness? Anger? Love? Attentively listen to each word you speak. If needed, remove some words from your vocabulary. Now replace them with life-giving words of love, respect, and praise.

Write out all the negative phrases you say. These possibly were planted in you when you were very young and the soil of your heart was fertile. Possibly words were said to you by someone in authority. Now, beside each phrase write what G-D says. In G-D's economy, if you say you are afraid, He says, "I have not given you a spirit of fear" (see 2 Tim. 1:7). If you say, "I can't," He says, "You can do all things" (see Phil. 4:13). If you say, "It's impossible." He says, "All things are possible" (see Luke 18:27).

_____

_____

2. When you observe your own driveway, you realize some roots can break through concrete or macadam; you too must be strengthened for your own breakthrough. Your only Source of strength is the Lord (see Ps. 28:7). Say it aloud with me: my *only* Source of strength is the Lord! Your light Source is Messiah Yeshua. Your water Source is the Word of G-D. G-D the Father is your Gardener (see John 15:1). Today, make a schedule and a time slot to be watered daily; find a time to read and meditate on G-D's Word. Also, schedule a time of prayer for others, Israel, and yourself with G-D the Father. Finally, spend every remaining space in your day with Yeshua. He is the living G-D who desires your complete attention. Invite Him along on your golf outing, your grocery run, and as you relax in your down time.

_____

_____

3. Are you persistent even in the little things? It's easy to fight for a cause for your school-age child when he or she has been wronged. But when you encounter that person who "stole your parking space" in the public parking lot, do you smile and gladly relinquish it to the person? We encounter

"concrete" (those with hard hearts) daily. Your rebuttal of kindness, helpfulness, or generosity may be enough to jolt them out of their negative emotion or angered mental state if even for a moment. Daily, plan to mete out three random acts of kindness. Next month, multiply your generosity to six or a dozen times. Conquer the "concrete" in your path with godly attributes and with the mind of Messiah.

---

4. The root seeks, grows toward, and—after overcoming every obstacle—reaches the water source. Imagine what that would look like to you and me in our lives. All our schedules would be secondary to spending time with the Lord. As hard hearts are encountered, we would forsake our schedule and take a detour from our usual route to make an extra effort. Visit the shut-in with soup in hand. Our priorities would be turned around; and if we did make it to our place of business, we would not commence working until we spent time ministering to the co-worker beside us. Or we might take more than the allotted time with the unsatisfied customer on the phone. Pick a day this week and realign your priorities. Call this your "G-D Day."

---

5. Close your eyes for just a moment and try to identify the anchors in your life. Is your anchor a person? Is it your education or background? Roots are the anchors for the tree. Yeshua wants to be your only anchor. Write out below your current

anchors and ask Yeshua if He would be the Anchor instead of these things. His answer is yes. He sent the *Ruach HaKodesh* (Holy Spirit) to help, guide, and inform (see John 14:16; 16:13).

_____

_____

_____

6. For believers in Messiah Yeshua, growth can be painful. Gaining knowledge in the Word is not growth. Application, experience, and wisdom in handling Bible knowledge is growth. Have you had an emergency situation, lifestyle change, or loss in the last year or in years past? How did you handle it? Would you handle things differently based on what you now know? Do your fears (if any) today exceed the fears you had in the past? Your fears should lessen over the years and not increase. Fear is unbelief in disguise. On a percentage scale from 0 to 100 percent, calculate your spiritual growth rate from one year ago to today. What is your growth rate between today and five years ago? Use the chart to determine your growth over the past years.

EVENT	GROWTH OVER ONE YEAR	GROWTH OVER FIVE YEARS
Increase in Bible knowledge		
Increase in talking about Messiah Yeshua		
Number of fears diminished		
Breakthroughs come when needed		
Ability to handle during lifecycle changes (death, job/address change, birth, etc.)		
Time between break downs, anger bursts, or need to run or hide increased		

EVENT	GROWTH OVER ONE YEAR	GROWTH OVER FIVE YEARS
Increase in daily prayer and meditation time		
Answered prayers happen more frequently		
Increase in faith even in the little things		

Average your scores and put the total here: _____. If you are 50 percent or above, you are in a growth spurt! Do not be discouraged over a lower score. You may be a late bloomer! The root system on a tree is complicated, and each system is unique. The next time a trial finds you, check your reaction toward it. Gauge your reaction against how you responded in years past. Do you see growth?

_____

_____

_____

7. To soar higher in any aspect of your life, you must go deeper. Plant yourself in the Word. Surround yourself with strong faith-filled believers in Messiah Yeshua. Pray always about everything. To prevent becoming root bound and to prevent root rot, join a new Bible study, acquire a mentor or become a mentor, and expand your knowledge of G-D in new and different ways. Write an idea or two that you have never tried regarding Bible-based growth. Then do it.

_____

_____

_____

THE TRUNK

Chapter 4

THE TRUNK

ONE OF THE MOST interesting parts of the English language is the cross usage of the same words used to mean different things based on the context. Hidden within these usages are some often subtle connections that are not as random as they initially appear. As we take our study of the tree up from the ground, we encounter the trunk.

My car has a trunk, an elephant has a trunk, my body is called my trunk, and my parents used to ship my clothes to summer camp in a trunk. All these references share something in common. The trunk is where things are stored and protected for either immediate or later use.

There are five layers to a tree trunk. And it's the tree's trunk that is the main support for the tree. The different parts of the trunk allow the tree to grow tall and sturdy, and provide a way for water and nutrients to flow from the roots to the leaves. Each part of the trunk serves a distinct purpose, working together to make the tree stronger.

The bark of the tree is the most recognized part of the trunk. It is the outermost layer and is comprised of dead cells that form a hard coating to protect the rest of the trunk. Bark characteristics differ for each tree species, and those characteristics help in tree identification. Phloem is the inner bark of the tree. Found just behind the outer bark, the phloem carries the food supply of sap to the rest of the tree, according to the North Carolina Forestry Association. The cambium, a single layer of living cells, is what produces the inner bark and the sapwood. Most active during the spring and summer months, the cambium causes the tree to grow in diameter. This growth causes rings inside the trunk to appear with each new season.

Sapwood is one of the two parts that make up the inner part of the trunk. These three parts together form the xylem. Sapwood is the outermost part of the xylem and brings water and nutrients from the roots to the rest of the tree. As the tree grows, the sapwood cells die off, and these dead cells form the heartwood. Heartwood is the second part of the xylem. Located in the very center of the tree, heartwood is darker than sapwood because of all the sugar and dyes stored in the cells.

As we look at the body of the tree, we see how similar it is to our own bodies. We also have an outer bark of skin that protects us from the elements. We also have a heart—a heartwood—that provides nutrition and pumps blood to all the extremities. We have a complex system inside of us in the same way that a tree in its trunk has a complex system inside of it. All the parts of the tree must work together for the tree to grow and remain strong. In the same way, our major organs must work in complete unity for us to be healthy. One part is no more important than another part.

> *For just as the body is one and has many parts, and all the parts of the body—though many—are one body, so also is Messiah. For in one Spirit we were all immersed*

*into one body—whether Jewish or Greek, slave or free—
and all were made to drink of one Spirit.*

*For the body is not one part, but many. If the foot says,
"Since I'm not a hand, I'm not part of the body," is it
therefore not part of the body? And if the ear says, "Since
I'm not an eye, I'm not part of the body," is it for this
reason any less part of the body? If the whole body were
an eye, where would the hearing be? If the whole were
hearing, where would the sense of smell be? But now G-D
has placed the parts—each one of them—in the body just
as He desired. If they were all one part, where would the
body be? But now there are many parts, yet one body.*

*The eye cannot tell the hand, "I don't need you!" or in turn
the head to the feet, "I don't need you!" On the contrary,
those parts of the body that seem to be less important are
indispensable. Those parts of the body that we think to
be less honorable, we clothe with greater honor; and our
unpresentable parts are treated with greater modesty; but
our presentable parts have no such need. Rather G-D
assembled the body, giving more honor to those who are
lacking, so that there may be no division in the body, but
so that the parts may have the same care for one another.
If one part suffers, all the parts suffer together. If one
part is honored, all the parts rejoice together.*

*Now you are the body of Messiah, and members individ-
ually. G-D has put into His community first shlichim,
second prophets, third teachers, then miracles, then heal-
ings, helps, leadership, various kinds of tongues. All are
not shlichim, are they? All are not prophets, are they?
All are not teachers, are they? All do not work miracles,*

do they? All do not have gifts of healing, do they? All do not speak in tongues, do they? All do not interpret, do they? But earnestly desire the greater gifts. And still I show you a far better way (1 Cor. 12:12-31).

Like the tree, our own bodies can be used for good or for evil. We can dedicate ourselves to the carnal life or the holy life. We can build synagogues and churches out of the same wood that we use to build crack houses. G-D separated the clean from the unclean, the holy from the profane. And just like our bodies, which can be used for G-D's Kingdom and for G-D's good, or can be used as the hand of evil and self-destruction, so the tree and the trunk of the tree can be used for good or for evil.

The carpenter measures with a line and makes an outline with a marker; he roughs it out with chisels and marks it with compasses. He shapes it in the form of man, of man in all his glory, that it may dwell in a shrine. He cut down cedars, or perhaps took a cypress or oak. He let it grow among the trees of the forest, or planted a pine, and the rain made it grow. It is man's fuel for burning; some of it he takes and warms himself, he kindles a fire and bakes bread. But he also fashions a god and worships it; he makes an idol and bows down to it. Half of the wood he burns in the fire; over it he prepares his meal, he roasts his meat and eats his fill. He also warms himself and says, "Ah! I am warm; I see the fire."

From the rest he makes a god, his idol; he bows down to it and worships. He prays to it and says, "Save me; you are my god." They know nothing, they understand nothing; their eyes are plastered over so they cannot see, and their minds closed so they cannot understand. No one stops

to think, no one has the knowledge or understanding to
say, "Half of it I used for fuel; I even baked bread over its
coals, I roasted meat and I ate. Shall I make a detestable
thing from what is left? Shall I bow down to a block of
wood?" He feeds on ashes, a deluded heart misleads him;
he cannot save himself, or say, "Is not this thing in my
right hand a lie?" (Isa. 44:13-20)

As we explore the connection between the tree and ourselves, we see how difficult it is to live in both worlds, the holy and the profane. Half the tree is used for cooking and warmth, and the other half for carving an idol. How easy it is to justify our behavior and rationalize what we do. G-D can only use clean vessels to bring about real transformation. We must be transformed into a new creation. We cannot change our bodies—in the same way that the tree cannot change its wood—but we can change the application of the resources G-D has created.

Since your body is the temple of the Lord, it must be kept from being defiled by the things of the world: *"Or don't you know that your body is a temple of the Ruach ha-Kodesh who is in you, whom you have from G-D, and that you are not your own? For you were bought with a price. Therefore glorify G-D in your body"* (1 Cor. 6:19-20). Further, as we examine the very specific instructions for the Tabernacle, that Holy Place in which G-D Himself dwelt among the children of Israel for 40 years in the desert, we begin to see that G-D wants us to follow a pattern. This is the only way we can prepare the place in which the *Ruach HaKodesh*, the Holy Spirit, can dwell.

In Exodus 25:8-16, we read the instructions from G-D:

Then have them make a sanctuary for Me, and I will dwell among them. Make this tabernacle and all its furnishings exactly like the pattern I will show you.

Have them make a chest of acacia wood—two and a half cubits long, a cubit and a half wide, and a cubit and a half high. Overlay it with pure gold, both inside and out, and make gold molding around it. Cast four gold rings for it and fasten them to four feet, with two rings on one side and two rings on the other side. Then make poles of acacia wood and overlay them with gold. Insert the poles into the rings in the side of the chest to carry it. The poles are to remain on the rings of this ark; they are not to be removed. Then put in the ark the Testimony, which I will give you.

G-D Himself supervised the selection of the materials of the Ark of the Covenant. They were assembled according to the will of G-D, thereby creating a holy place for the natural objects of G-D to reside. He would place in there the Ten Commandments, the budding staff of Aaron, and the golden jar of manna. Moses' instructions were to create a holy vessel according to His pattern so that holy objects could be placed in it without being defiled.

G-D gave similar instructions when He supervised the building of the Temple that would bear His name. In Second Chronicles 2:8-9, Solomon, working with the blueprint the Lord had given his father David, sent this message to the king of Tyre:

Send me also cedar, pine and algum logs from Lebanon, for I know that your men are skilled in cutting timber there. My men will work with yours to provide me with plenty of lumber, because the temple I build must be large and magnificent.

The trunk of that tree was used to make things that are holy. Sadly, the same wood was used to make both holy vessels and idols that were detestable to G-D. In Deuteronomy 16:21-22, the Lord said, *"Do not set up any wooden Asherah pole beside the altar you build to the Lord your G-D, and do not erect a sacred stone, for these the Lord your G-D hates."* And in First Kings 16:33, *"Ahab also made an Asherah pole and did more to provoke the Lord, the G-D of Israel, to anger Him than did all the kings of Israel before him."* For it was detestable to take this sacred element, this life that G-D gave us in the tree, and make something detestable to G-D.

The wood for these vessels and the wood for these idols were no different. The difference between one purpose being clean and another profane was in the hands of the user. We, like the lumber contained in the trunk of the tree, can be used for whatever we purpose. The potential for good and evil applications lies in our hands, not in the wood itself.

As we examine the trunk of the tree, we also see that each species of tree has a trunk specifically suited to its environment. The pine grows tall and slender to rise above the shorter, more sturdy hardwoods as it fights for its survival. The palm has a fibrous, flexible trunk able to withstand the high winds characteristic of its environment. The oak grows broad and thick with spreading branches and establishes itself to dominate its space. It is more rigid, but with a lower center of gravity to resist the onslaught of seasonal storms.

When you look at the trees, which one do you identify with? Are you like the oak tree whose wood is hard and whose trunk is thick? When the wind blows, it does not budge, but remains so rigid in its stance that there comes a point when it must break or be uprooted. Or are you like the palm that soars to great heights? In dry conditions, its roots may have more mass than its trunk, and in wet conditions maybe only three feet deep—but when the storm comes, it remains flexible and survives even hurricane force winds.

Who will you be? How deep will you put your roots, and in what kind of ground will you plant? And what seeds have you planted in your life that will come forth in due season? Will you be like the rigid oak that has majesty and beauty, but is so rigid in its structure that when the winds of change come, it stands there unable to bend? You have no doubt seen the damage after tornadoes and storms pass through; beautiful 200 and 300-year-old oak trees lie fractured and broken, uprooted because they had no flexibility. They completely resisted to the point of breaking.

Or will you be like the palm tree that grows to great heights, whose root system is complex yet simply seeks water? When the wind comes, it bows and bends, but change does not break it. Have you seen video on television or the Internet of the hurricanes in Florida and the winds blowing and the palms tree swaying—almost bending in half, but not breaking? Against hurricane force winds, they still were not uprooted. In their resilience and ability to bend with the force of nature, they found security and safety.

When we look at our bodies, we realize that although we ask the *Ruach HaKodesh* (the Holy Spirit) to come into our hearts, it is our innermost parts, our trunk, where He resides, according to John 7:38-39:

> *"Whoever believes in Me, as the Scripture says, 'out of his innermost being will flow rivers of living water.'"*
> *Now He said this about the Ruach, whom those who trusted in Him were going to receive; for the Ruach was not yet given, since Yeshua was not yet glorified.*

When we come up against the pressures of the world and compromise and bend at our trunks, we are bending and compromising the very place in which the Holy Spirit resides. This may be a survival technique for the tree, but this bending becomes a breaking point for us. G-D wants us to hold firm in our faith and resist the pressures and the temptations that come against us. His Word says:

> Therefore submit to G-D. But resist the devil and he will flee from you. Draw near to G-D, and He will draw near to you. Cleanse your hands, you sinners, and purify your hearts, you double-minded! Lament and mourn and weep! Let your laughter be turned into mourning, and your joy into gloom. Humble yourselves in the sight of ADONAI, and He shall lift you up (James 4:7-10)

It was the trunk of the tree that was used to make the ark that G-D instructed Noah to build. It was the trunk of the tree that was used to make the altar of incense, the table of showbread, the brazen altar, and the uprights for the tabernacle. And it was the trunk of the tree that was used to make the cross that Yeshua was sacrificed upon.

SEVEN LESSONS LEARNED FROM THE TRUNK

1. Like our bodies, the trunk of the tree houses the internal systems that feed and nourish the limbs. We must be careful to take care of our bodies, for they are the temple of the Lord. All the parts matter, and neglecting one has an impact on the others. All the parts must work in complete harmony for us to be at optimum health.

2. The trunk can be used for both the clean and the profane. Each one of us has a purpose, and we must be intentional about how we are being used. If we follow G-D's instructions, only good will come from our bodies and the Body of Messiah. If what we are doing or being asked to do does not line up with the Word of G-D, then it is clear that it is not His will.

3. If the tree remains too rigid, it will break or be uprooted. If we remain too rigid and fail to find a good balance, we too can break or be uprooted. We must be uncompromising about the things of G-D, but remain flexible so that we are not overcome with pride. Our way is not the only way, and we must be sensitive to the needs of others. Above all, we need to be mindful of the words of James 4:7: *"Therefore submit to G-D. But resist the devil and he will flee from you."* In our resistance we will be met with the utmost support from G-D who will uphold us with His outstretched right hand.

4. If you cut or burn the bark of the trunk, it will bear an external reminder of that cut. But if you cut or burn the heartwood, the tree may be wounded beyond recovery. Choose your words carefully. that they do not cut to the heart of another. According to James 3:6, the *"tongue is a fire. The tongue is a world of evil placed among our body parts.... And Proverbs 12:18 says, "Reckless words pierce like a sword, but the tongue of the wise brings healing."*

5. The careful carpenter uses the right tools and the right wood for the job. He measures twice and cuts once. So, too, we are to listen twice as much as we speak. Proverbs 18:13 says, *"He who answers before listening—that is his folly and his shame.* And Jesus said,*"For with the judgment you judge, you will be judged; and with the measure you use, it will be measured to you"* (Matt. 7:2).

6. Just as the bark of the trunk is for protection against the elements, pests, disease, and infection, so we must be tough skinned and not allow any offense to take hold. We must refrain from gossip and slander and planting seeds of discord. *"Without wood a fire goes out; without gossip a quarrel dies down"* (Prov. 26:20).

7. The same tree that in the form of a cross has become a stumbling block has also become the altar of our salvation. What the enemy means for evil, G-D will work for His glory!

MAIN FRAME

For the message of the cross is foolishness to those who are perishing, but to us who are being saved it is the power of G-D. For it is written, "I will destroy the wisdom of the wise and bring to nothing the understanding of the intelligent." Where is the wise one? Where is the Torah scholar? Where is the debater of this age? Hasn't G-D made foolish the wisdom of the world? For seeing that—in G-D's wisdom—the world through its wisdom did not know G-D, G-D was pleased—through the foolishness of the message proclaimed—to save those who believe. For Jewish people ask for signs and Greek people seek after wisdom, but we proclaim Messiah crucified—a stumbling block to Jewish people and foolishness to Gentile people, but to those who are called (both Jewish and Greek people), Messiah, the power of G-D and the wisdom of G-D. For the foolishness of G-D is wiser than men, and the weakness of G-D is stronger than men.

For you see your calling, brothers and sisters, that not many are wise according to human standards, not many are powerful, and not many are born well. Yet G-D chose the foolish things of the world so He might put to shame the wise; and G-D chose the weak things of the world so He might put to shame the strong; and G-D chose the lowly and despised things of the world, the things that are as nothing, so He might bring to nothing the things that are—so that no human might boast before G-D. But because of Him you are in Messiah Yeshua, who became to us wisdom from G-D and righteousness and holiness and redemption—so that, just as it is written, "Let him who boasts, boast in ADONAI" (1 Cor. 1:18-31).

This passage in First Corinthians refers to the sacrifice stake, the cross, made out of lumber from the trunk of the tree—the same wooden stake the lamb was placed upon in the home during the first Passover. This wooden stake is referred to in the Hebrew as an *Etz*, a tree. It is no coincidence that Yeshua, like Isaac, carried the wood (*etz*) for His sacrifice up the hill. And, as is always the case in G-D's economy, what is begun in the Old Covenant is fulfilled in the New. Isaac was redeemed by the lamb of G-D provided for on Mount Moriah, and now all mankind is redeemed by the Lamb of G-D sacrificed on a tree once for all mankind. It was through this sacrifice on that wooden altar that the Levitical system of sacrifice was fulfilled and finished. Without a sacrifice, there is no forgiveness for sins. We cannot redeem ourselves—neither in the Old Covenant nor in the New.

How can we be forgiven? How can we be redeemed? There is only one way, and that is to accept the atonement made through Yeshua—to believe that the sacrifice tree that held His body has become the *Etz Chaim*, the Tree of Life. Pray with me now: "Lord, I'm sorry. I'm sorry I've sinned against You. And I believe Yeshua died for my sins, and on the third day He rose again, and because He is sitting at the right hand of Your throne, Father, and because He lives, I can live today."

BODY BUILDING

1. What does it mean to regard your body as the temple of the *Ruach HaKodesh* (see 1 Cor. 6:19)? The *Ruach* is spirit and does not depend on carnal or natural things. He requires nourishment from G-D's Word. He depends on your right attitude and love. Additionally, when you exhibit love to others, the *Ruach* is fed. List the ways you communicate G-D's love (see 1 Cor. 13:4-8) List new ways in which you can and will show love today.

---

2. Even when you are right, you can be wrong. Each time you argue, forcibly correct, or push your ideas and agendas on others, you are not walking in love. First John 4:16 says, *"So we have come to know and trust in the love that G-D has for us. G-D is love. Now whoever abides in love abides in G-D, and G-D abides*

in him." As a temple for the *Ruach HaKodesh,* are you supplying proper nourishment to Him? Your words have the power to bless or to curse. And Proverbs 18:21 says, *"The tongue has the power of life and death…"* Write a description of the last argument you "won." Now, consider the opposing person. Did they feel defeated? Corrected? Bullied? Take time to confess, repent, and say a blessing for the offended person(s).

_____

_____

_____

3. Are you like the oak tree that is too rigid or like the palm tree that gently bends even in the stormiest winds? Describe the tree that most resembles you and why.

_____

_____

_____

4. Are others ever offended by your words? Choose your words carefully, and choose the timing of their delivery more carefully. "Preach the gospel, and if necessary use words," this advice given by an unknown author is wisdom to be applied to everything "preached" and spoken. Pray for a guard over your mouth (see Ps. 141:3) each time you speak. Ask the Lord to bless the hearing and receiving of your words. What other ways can you protect against harming others with your words and gestures? Write at least three ways here.

_____

_____

_____

5. Communication is more than words spoken. You communicate through inflection, tone, and volume. Body language can be a powerful tool of communication. G-D considers haughty eyes an abomination (see Prov. 6:16-17). Repent for each time you use(d) any body part: eyes, fingers, tongue, hands, feet, etc., in any disrespectful gesture.

---

6. Before walking into an appointment, engagement, movie, and before taking or making a phone call, before watching television or having involvement in any activity, be sure to put on the full armor of G-D. Ephesians 6:14-17 says:

> *Buckle the belt of truth around your waist, and put on the breastplate of righteousness. Strap up your feet in readiness with the Good News of shalom. Above all, take up the shield of faith with which you will be able to extinguish all the flaming arrows of the evil one. And take the helmet of salvation and the sword of the Spirit, which is the word of G-D.*

Pray and visualize dressing in this armor regularly. Why regularly? Because our armor can become damaged from all the flaming arrows (persecution, curses, doubts, lies, false teachings, and impure ideas) the adversary shoots our way. Other than these instances, what activities do you find it necessary to first put on G-D's armor? Write your ideas.

---

7. When you receive bad news, allow yourself to:

- Believe Genesis 3: What the enemy means for evil, G-D will work for His glory.

- Pray Romans 8:28: In all things G-D works for the good of those who love Him.

- Rebuke what does not edify G-D, Israel, or you.

- Stand firm on G-D's Word and all Yeshua has accomplished.

THE BRANCHES

Chapter 5

THE BRANCHES

MANY CHILDHOOD MEMORIES ARE filled with images of tire swings and tree houses perched high above the ground. These were special places where peals of laughter could be heard around the neighborhood. Children skinned their knees climbing trees and still came back for more. Saturday afternoons and summer evenings were appointed times for gathering at the ginko or fig tree, more commonly referred to as the climbing tree.

What was it about those trees scattered across every urban and rural neighborhood around the world that cried out to kids from every walk of life? Sure, the trunk had to be climbable, but the real feature that captured the attention and the imagination of every child who gazed upon it were the branches. The upswept, outstretched arms of the tree that could support the weight of one or many called out with the words that every child longs to hear, "Climb me!"

Our journey above ground takes us up the trunk to the branches. As we move upward toward the branches, our climb is unencumbered, for the branches tend to grow at the top of the tree and form a crown. However, along the way, we may run into some branches that have grown abnormally along the trunk. These "sucker branches" tend to divert nutrients that are needed to nourish the top branches, but are hijacked along the way:

> You may have noticed that an odd branch has started growing from the base or the roots of your tree. It may look much like the rest of the plant, but soon it becomes apparent that this strange branch is nothing at all like the tree you planted. The leaves may look different, it may produce inferior fruit, or it may be a different kind of tree all together. What is going on? Your tree has developed a sucker. While you might be tempted to leave a tree sucker, remove it as quickly as possible. A tree sucker will sap the energy away from the healthier and more desirable branches on top. Chances are, you will not be pleased by the plant produced by the tree sucker. Remove them to improve the health of the plant overall.[1]

In our spiritual journey upward, there can be people who will latch onto us and become a drain and a distraction. The instructions for the removal of the branch that is a negative influence on the growth of tree states:

> Tree sucker removal is easy to do. Tree sucker removal is done in the same way pruning is. Using a sharp, clean pair of pruning shears, cleanly cut the plant sucker as close to the tree as possible, but leave the collar (where the tree sucker meets the tree) to help speed the wound recovery. Perform this tree sucker control as soon as you see any plant suckers appear so that you put less stress on your tree.[2]

Good advice for the tree and for ourselves.

A tree branch's job is to provide a way for the tree leaves to act as a net for sunlight. The branch will grow to give the most leaves the most light, even if that means growing sideways. There are other factors that affect the way branches grow as well. Gravity pulls the branches downward, and branch growth is affected by the wind. Part of the trade-off any tree has to make is between gathering light, staying stable in the wind, and succeeding against nearby competitors. Again we see the need for the balance between three elements forming a compound unity.

When a tree's branches grow crookedly, that's part of the tree's overall survival strategy. Trees have sensors that detect light and gravity. From the moment a tree begins its life, it knows which end is up. Trees will generally attempt to grow toward the light and away from gravitational pull. As a tree gets older, its branches tend to grow more outward than upward so the tree can cast a wider net to catch the light of the sun.

Branches unable to support themselves are sealed off, then die, and fall off the tree. Sealing off the weak branch from the rest of the tree insures the tree is protected against disease and insects. Branches on the interior of a shade tree that do not receive adequate light will die and eventually fall.

In our study of the tree, we begin to see that G-D has given us something physical and tangible, something we see every day to illustrate His presence and design, and in this study of the branches we see yet again what G-D is telling us about the supernatural as He shows us the natural. Just as Yeshua and the Father are one, G-D's plan has always been for us, through Him, to be one with Him.

Never asking anything from us, ever standing with arms raised as in praise, trees are still, for the most part, taken for granted. We pass by them every day. Some are majestic and some are scrawny. Some are beautiful, and their majesty is breathtaking. Others are ordinary, nondescript, and unattractive, yet they all contribute to the air we breathe. There is no correlation between their function and their beauty.

In this study on the tree, we began by looking at the ground, the very ground in which the tree grows in. Who of us can take that dust of the earth, breathe into it, and bring it to life? Who of us can create what G-D has created? Who of us can birth a tree? G-D has given us the tree, mentioned almost 600 times in Scripture. In fact, trees and wood are mentioned more often than any other living thing other than man. He wants us to look at the tree. He wants us to look at the Tree of Life and understand it.

Complex concepts require us to break them down into understandable parts so we can grasp their richness. G-D's Word is complex, and we must break it down into its component parts to study and understand it.

The branches of the tree provide for the catching of the sunlight so photosynthesis can begin. This becomes a source of life to the tree. In G-D's Word, He shows us that the Branch will be the Source of life to Israel, its people, and ultimately all mankind:

> *In that day the Branch of the Lord will be beautiful and glorious, and the fruit of the land will be the pride and the glory of the survivors in Israel* (Isa. 4:2).

> *"The days are coming," declares the Lord, "when I will raise up to David a righteous Branch; a King who will reign wisely and do what is just and right in the land. In His days Judah will be saved and Israel will live in*

safety. This is the name by which He will be called: The Lord Our Righteousness" (Jer. 23:5-6).

Tell him this is what the Lord Almighty says: "Here is the Man whose name is the Branch, and He will branch out from His place and build the temple of the Lord. It is He who will build the temple of the Lord, and He will be clothed with majesty and will sit and rule on His throne. And He will be a priest on His throne...." (Zech. 6:12-13).

John 15 tells us a story of the vine and the branches, a story which we must understand in our lives if we're to understand in the natural what G-D wants us to see in the supernatural. For who of us has not been pruned by the Lord, and who of us has not been disciplined? No discipline or pruning feels good at the time, but it's for one purpose only: to provide room for new growth. The Word of G-D says in John 15:1-8:

I am the true vine, and My Father is the gardener. Every branch in Me that does not bear fruit, He takes away; and every branch that bears fruit, He trims so that it may bear more fruit. You are already clean because of the word I have spoken to you. Abide in Me, and I will abide in you. The branch cannot itself produce fruit, unless it abides on the vine. Likewise, you cannot produce fruit unless you abide in Me.

I am the vine; you are the branches. The one who abides in Me, and I in him, bears much fruit; for apart from Me, you can do nothing. If anyone does not abide in Me, he is thrown away like a branch and is dried up. Such branches are picked up and thrown into the fire and burned.

If you abide in Me and My words abide in you, ask whatever you wish, and it shall be done for you. In this My Father is glorified, that you bear much fruit and so prove to be My disciples.

We are all *talmadim* (disciples). We are all disciples of G-D; and each one of us who has the Word of G-D, has good instruction.

Many years ago I attended a High Tech Prayer Breakfast in Atlanta, Georgia, and the teaching was on the book *Secrets of the Vine* by Bruce Wilkinson. The PowerPoint presentation that was used was so colorful and so thorough that I asked to borrow it so that I could present the same material at Congregation Beth Hallel in Roswell, Georgia. There is no doubt that Bruce Wilkinson's book and his insights on this lesson have greatly influenced this section on the branches.[3]

In the natural, there are many reasons why a tree does not bear fruit. If soil conditions are not right, the tree may not be receiving the right amounts or balance of nutrients. If there is too much or too little water, the tree may not bear fruit. Light, temperature, and pollutants can all impact the tree's ability to bear fruit.

Our lives are no different from the tree—and our ability to produce branches that yield fruit is directly proportionate to the positive and negative influences in our lives. If we are not bearing fruit, we can deduce that we are allowing negative influences to impact our lives. It may be toxic thinking or toxic behaviors. Or, it may simply be that we are in sin.

If there is sin G-D uses discipline to cut off the branch that is not producing fruit, but if your life is bearing fruit for the Lord, He will prune you to make room for new growth. A vine left untended will stop bearing fruit. It will grow wild, past the point of being productive. If our lives are not pruned to make room for new growth, we will stop bearing fruit.

We must look at the condition of our lives; if we are bearing no fruit or the fruit is not sweet, we need to take a look at the negative influences and stand against them. Whatever it is we're doing that is causing us not to bear fruit for G-D, we must stand against it. We must turn away from it. We must repent. We have to do an about-face so that we can begin to bear fruit. And if we are bearing fruit for the Lord, we must receive His pruning.

How do you think it feels to the rosebush when you come along with a pair of shears? "You're cutting off my limb; you're cutting off my branch; that hurts!" But next spring, look at the abundance of new growth. And hear how the rosebush looks at itself and says, "Look at me now. I'm the most beautiful in your garden. Look at me now."

It is the same with us when the time comes that we begin to bear much fruit for G-D because He's pruned us to bring about new fruit in our lives. We begin to feel good about the harvest. We forget about the pruning. But, I can assure you, that the next pruning will come, for if we're not growing, just like the tree, we're dying.

You cannot tell the difference between discipline and pruning by how you feel because neither one feels good. It's only by looking at the fruit in your life. If you're bearing no fruit, it's because your commitment to your sin is greater than your commitment to G-D's plan for your life.

I am often asked about how I came to know Yeshua as my Messiah. Although I did not know it at the time, there were those in my life who seemed to fully grasp Rabbi Shaul's (Paul's) message in Romans chapter 11. In this chapter, Rabbi Shaul clearly charges the Gentile believers in Yeshua to not take this gift of salvation for granted, but instead to provoke Israel to envy for the hope given to them. Up until this point, I can honestly say I was provoked, but not to envy! It was through the kindness and love of Messiah and sensitivity to my Jewishness that led me to the doors of Beth Hallel in Roswell, Georgia. It was there I learned for the first time that His name was Yeshua. He was Jewish. He was the Lamb of G-D who redeemed us on Mount Moriah, in Egypt, and finally on that sacrifice tree. They knew that I would never convert, never give up my Jewish identity, and yet they knew I needed Messiah.

As we read in Romans 11:11-12:

> *I say then, they did not stumble so as to fall, did they? May it never be! But by their false step salvation has come to the Gentiles, to provoke Israel to jealousy. Now if their transgression leads to riches for the world, and their loss riches for the Gentiles, then how much more their fullness!*

This fullness Paul speaks of in Romans 11 is the fullness of Messiah in our lives. It is the fullness of G-D's presence. It is the fullness of the Holy Spirit taking up residence within us. This is the fullness G-D is referring to. This fullness comes when Messiah is so alive in us that there is more of Him and less of us to the point we come to the end of ourselves.

Rabbi Shaul goes on to say:

> *But I am speaking to you who are Gentiles. Insofar as I am a shaliach to the Gentiles, I spotlight my ministry if somehow I might provoke to jealousy my own flesh and blood and save some of them. For if their rejection leads*

to the reconciliation of the world, what will their accep-
tance be but life from the dead?

If the firstfruit is holy, so is the whole batch of dough; and
if the root is holy, so are the branches. But if some of the
branches were broken off and you—being a wild olive—
were grafted in among them and became a partaker of
the root of the olive tree with its richness, do not boast
against the branches. But if you do boast, it is not you
who support the root but the root supports you. You will
say then, "Branches were broken off so that I might be
grafted in." True enough. They were broken off because
of unbelief, and you stand by faith. Do not be arrogant,
but fear—for if G-D did not spare the natural branches,
neither will He spare you (Rom. 11:13-21).

In the world today, millions are being taught that the Church replaced Israel. This replacement theology is anti-Semitism at its very core. If G-D could break His covenant with Israel, what makes you think He wouldn't break His covenant with you? If He would break His promises to Israel, the apple of His eye, what makes them think that the Church matters more than Israel? Or that the Church would matter more than the place of the return of Messiah?

The branches do not support the root. The root supports the branches. When you really grasp this grafting-in concept, you understand that I, as a Jew, am a natural branch cut off for unbelief, but grafted in to the same tree that Gentile believers are grafted into. When we understand the role of the branches to provoke Israel to envy, we bring about supernatural change. When we join together as *Am Echad*—one people—we draw upon the power of unity. It's not a one or the other; it's one and the other standing together, shoulder to shoulder. For in G-D's Kingdom in the Spirit, there is no Greek and there is no Jew; there is no male and female. G-D didn't make a mistake when He made you Jewish, and G-D didn't make a mistake when He made you Gentile. He called all of us together for such a time as this. For if G-D did not spare the natural branches, He will not spare you either.

In Romans 11:22-24, Rabbi Shaul speaks clearly to this issue:

> Notice then the kindness and severity of G-D: severity toward those who fell; but G-D's kindness toward you, if you continue in His kindness; otherwise you too will be cut off! And they also, if they do not continue in their unbelief, will be grafted in; for G-D is able to graft them in again. For if you were cut out of that which by nature is a wild olive tree, and grafted contrary to nature into a cultivated olive tree, how much more will these natural branches be grafted into their own olive tree?

The commonwealth of Israel is an olive tree rich with grafted-in branches. In Ephesians 2:11-22, we read about this one new man:

> Therefore, keep in mind that once you—Gentiles in the flesh—were called "uncircumcision" by those called "circumcision" (which is performed on flesh by hand). At that time you were separate from Messiah, excluded from the commonwealth of Israel and strangers to the covenants of promise, having no hope and without G-D in the world. But now in Messiah Yeshua, you who once were far off have been brought near by the blood of the Messiah. For He is our shalom, the One who made the

two into one and broke down the middle wall of separation. Within His flesh He made powerless the hostility— the law code of mitzvot contained in regulations. He did this in order to create within Himself one new man from the two groups, making shalom, and to reconcile both to G-D in one body through the cross—by which He put the hostility to death. And He came and proclaimed shalom to you who were far away and shalom to those who were near—for through Him we both have access to the Father by the same Spirit. So then you are no longer strangers and foreigners, but you are fellow citizens with G-D's people and members of G-D's household. You have been built on the foundation made up of the shlichim and prophets, with Messiah Yeshua Himself being the cornerstone. In Him the whole building, being fitted together, is growing into a holy temple for the Lord. In Him, you also are being built together into G-D's dwelling place in the Spirit.

SEVEN LESSONS LEARNED FROM THE BRANCHES

1. The tree and its branches know which way is up from the very beginning of its life. It spends its entire life seeking new heights, even defying gravity. We too must demonstrate the commitment of the branches to resist the pull of the world and seek new heights in Him.

2. Like the branches, if we do not receive adequate light (Yeshua), we will die and eventually fall. All the darkness in the world cannot extinguish the light of even one small candle.

3. From humble beginnings as a seed, a tree will grow forth, and its branches will become a resting place for many. So too we cannot despise the day of small beginnings and must press on to the mark of the high calling of Messiah—for us as a Body to become a resting place for many. It is under the shelter of the branches that we find our safety.

4. Apart from the tree, the branch can do nothing. Branches that cannot support themselves are sealed off from the nourishing sap and fall to the ground to decay. Separation from G-D and doing things in our own will yield the same results.

5. Any branch that does not bear fruit is cut off and thrown into the fire. We must bear fruit in order to remain an active part of the tree. Not only are we to bear fruit by sharing the Good News of Messiah, we are also to bear all the fruit of the Spirit: *"love, joy, peace, patience, kindness, goodness, faithfulness, gentleness, and self-control"* (Gal. 5:22-23).

6. Branches must be pruned to make room for new growth. If they are bearing fruit before they are pruned, they will bear more after the pruning. If we are to bear much fruit, we also need to be pruned. We must be willing to be refined and feel the sharp shears of the One who will prune us so that we may bear much fruit for His Kingdom.

7. Branches can be grafted into a tree and can receive nourishment from the root, but the branches do not support the root. The root supports
the branches. For us to make a real difference in
G-D's Kingdom, we must share together in the
rich roots of Israel, our Jewish heritage, so that
we, Jew and Gentile, may become one in Messiah
to make Israel envious enough to cry out, *"Baruch
haba B'Shem Adonai, blessed is He who comes in the
name of the Lord."*

OUT ON A LIMB

We've been talking about the tree. And no branch on its own
can do anything separated from the tree. It can bear no fruit. It
cannot continue with its life; and any branch that is cut off, will
be thrown into the fire. G-D gives us this example to show us
that in and of ourselves we can accomplish nothing. We are only
fruitful as we are attached to Him, our Source of life. The Tree
of Life—the branch that He said would come—is Yeshua. He
said there will come forth a rod out of Jesse, a branch will grow
from its root. Yeshua was that Branch that G-D spoke about. He
said, "Abide in Me, and I will abide in you" (see John 15).

What does it mean *to abide?* It means to remain, to dwell, to
tabernacle, to be in His presence, to invite Him into our lives so
that we would do more with Him. G-D has a plan. His plan is
for life, not for death. It's not His desire to cut off any branch
and throw it in the fire. G-D has laid out for us His perfect will.
We tend to hang out in His permissive will, but G-D wants each
and every one of us to draw closer to Him, to abide in Him
so He may abide in us. He is calling us to enter into His presence, not just once a week on Shabbat, but to enter in and just

stay there, to draw upon the nourishing sap, the living water that flows into and up through the roots and to the branches through the Branch, Messiah.

You may say, "Rabbi, what do I have to do to abide in Him? I don't get it. I don't understand. How do I abide in something? How do I remain in something?" It is the same way you remain up in the tree. You grab hold of the Branch. Yeshua is the Branch G-D spoke of. He is the One written about in the Hebrew Scriptures. He is Messiah, and no one comes to the Father but through the Son. This is G-D's plan.

If we have really come to the end of ourselves, that is where He can begin. We must grab hold of the Branch. Change will come. Fruit will come into your life. Your attitude about your life will change. Your attitude about your circumstances will change. Yeshua said there will be tribulation. This is no easy ride. But the Word of G-D says count it all joy (see James 1:2). Whatever trials you go through are only temporary. This is not your home. This is not where you will remain forever. Heaven is remaining in the presence of G-D forever, and hell is eternal separation from G-D. There's Heaven to gain, and there's a hell to shun. For some people, this life we live is the only hell that they'll ever know. And for others, this is the only Heaven.

This is how we abide in Him: when we come to a point where we know that we can do nothing without Him. He is the Creator; we are the creation, and we need Him. We need His plan. You say, "Well, how do I do that, Rabbi? How do I abide in Him?" This is how—you say, "Lord, I'm sorry I sinned against You. I ask Yeshua into my heart, and I believe that He died for my sins and that through His shed blood I am forgiven. I believe He died on that sacrifice tree and on the third day He rose again, and He's sitting at the right hand of G-D interceding for me. And because He lives I can have life eternal."

BRANCHING OUT

1. Proverbs 29:18 states that without a vision the people perish. Write a personal vision for your life. Include your Kingdom work in the vision. Think past what you may accomplish over the next decades and seek G-D's heart to discover that godly person you and G-D desire you to be.

_____

_____

_____

2. Look at your vision composed above. How much does it resemble Yeshua? To live, talk, and walk as He did requires us to be in His presence more often than not. Best friends look and dress alike because they desire to be alike. Intentionally, make Yeshua your Best Friend. Invite Him to ride along in the car with you and tell Him the gamut of things you think about ,from exciting to scary. What qualities do you want in a best friend? Write them. Then, check to see which ones you already have in Him.

_____

_____

_____

3. You were born a tiny baby, not a full-grown adult. Many projects and ideas have humble beginnings. Dedicate each idea and each project you have to the Lord; and, as obstacles arise, turn to Him in prayer for answers (see Jer. 33:3). Meditate and

ask the Lord to reveal a fresh idea to you. Then dedicate it back to Him and ask for His protection and provision. Obey as He guides you through each step or asks you to wait. Journal your ideas, and journal the steps taken from beginning to end.

_____

_____

_____

_____

_____

4. Secular people are everywhere. List the places where you encounter nonbelievers. The next time you plan to see these people, say a short prayer beforehand and ask G-D to go before you (see Isa. 45:2). Ask Him to fill your mouth with His words and your mind with His thoughts. Then, as you leave, ask Him to protect you from behind (see Isa. 58:8). Write the outcome of this experiment and be encouraged to repeat when necessary.

_____

_____

_____

5. Congregational meetings are biblical (see Heb. 10:25) and healthy to your soul and your spirit. The next time you are at services, forget about your needs and find three people to bless if even in a small way. Perhaps a widow hasn't received a hug since last week—give her a hug! It could also be that a young couple with children hasn't had alone time since last weekend. Invite them to a quiet dinner or offer them a gift card for a date night. In what other ways can you reach out to the needs of your congregation?

---

6. Pruning and discipline can feel the same. How do you know the difference? You may never know one from the other, but be encouraged just the same. G-D loves you enough to prune you even in a growing season. His desire is that you produce abundant fruit. His desire is for you to be used in His Kingdom. And His desire is that you witness to those who do not know Yeshua as Messiah so that none should perish (see 2 Pet. 3:9). Humble yourself and ask the Lord to show you where He wants new growth in your life. Then allow Him to cut away the needless things for new growth to begin. List any areas where pruning or discipline is needed in your life.

---

7. As a believer you are adopted by Him as His child, and as a non-Jewish believer you are grafted into the Olive Tree. As a Jewish person, you too are grafted into the Olive Tree upon submitting to the Jewish Messiah (see Rom. 10:9). Now that this has happened, you must go to that Tree, Yeshua, for nourishment. Any other supply of nourishment will leave you unsatisfied and malnourished. All other nourishment is false. Create a system for recognizing when you are empty and in need of nourishment. Record five "red flags" that signal your need for spiritual food.

ENDNOTES

1. See http://www.gardeningknowhow.com/trees-shrubs/tree -sucker-removal-and-tree-sucker-control.htm; accessed January 26, 2012.

2. Ibid.

3. Bruce Wilkinson, *Secrets of the Vine* (Sisters, OR: Multnomah, 2001).

THE
LEAVES

Chapter 6

THE LEAVES

AGAIN WE JOURNEY INTO the creative nature of the English language as we explore the Lessons Learned from the Leaf. When we take an extended period of time off of work, we are on a leave of absence. When we want to expand a table, we add a leaf. The act of exiting from a room is called leaving.

Of course, the leaf that we are exploring here is the foliage of the tree. And when we refer to it as foliage, we are looking at it in a plural sense since one leaf on its own cannot contribute significantly to the health of the tree. It, like us, compounds its effectiveness when working in a larger group in a unified effort to support the tree, and in turn the environment in which we live.

In the world of trees, as in our world, looks can be deceiving. Dead and dormant can look the same when it comes to trees. Never mind the type of tree or the time of year, you just can't really tell if a tree is dead or alive from its appearance alone. Logically, we can assume that if it is winter the tree is dormant, but we have no concrete evidence until spring. The prime indicator of life is the bud that starts out as a mere bump on the branch. Just as the life that begins inside the womb is small, so too the outgrowth that appears on the branch as a small bump harbors a life within and soon comes bursting forth. The leaf breaks forth and unfurls itself to provide a unique shape designed for gathering sunlight. Like us, it is created with veins; and through those veins, life-sustaining nutrients are circulated to the tree. The size and shape of the leaf are uniquely designed to produce the most effective use of the environment in which the tree grows. Some are flat and long while others can be short and wide.

Leaves, like every part of the tree, have a function and a purpose. Their purpose is to gather sunlight for photosynthesis. During this process of converting nutrients into sugar to feed the tree, the leaf absorbs carbon dioxide, and then it expels oxygen for us to breathe. We have a symbiotic relationship with the tree and its leaves as we cannot live without oxygen. Not only do leaves produce oxygen for us to breathe, they also absorb pollutants and impurities as they help clean the air. Leaves of certain trees can be used for food—not only for animals, but also for us—and many leaves are used for medicinal purposes.

> *Fruit trees of all kinds will grow on both banks of the river. Their leaves will not wither, nor will their fruit fail. Every month they will bear, because the water from the sanctuary flows to them. Their fruit will serve for food and their **leaves for healing** (Ezek. 47:12).*

> *...And the **leaves** of the tree **were for the healing** of the nations (Rev. 22:2).*

During their life cycle, leaves also fall to the earth, die, and return precious minerals, salts, and nutrients stored in their cells back into the soil. What was originally produced by the tree now enhances the ground beneath the tree, and the cycle begins again. Like man, they return to their very origin.

Throughout the ages there have been many stories that capture G-D's immeasurable concern for life. I particularly like those of the many Jewish sages who impart great wisdom and see G-D's plan in even the most common of activities. As I read the following story, I saw clearly that even the smallest leaf matters to G-D and His majesty is revealed in all things.

> As a young boy, Rabbi Yosef Yitzchak (the sixth Lubavitcher Rebbe) would go with his father on walks through the woods. One time, as they talked, the boy absent-mindedly plucked a leaf off a tree and began to shred it between his fingers. His father saw what his son was doing, but he went on talking. He spoke about the Baal Shem Tov, who taught how every leaf that blows in the wind—moving to the right and then to the left, how and when it falls and where it falls to—every motion for the duration of its existence is under the detailed supervision of the Almighty. That concern the Creator has for each thing, his father explained, is the divine spark that sustains its existence. Everything is with Divine purpose, everything is of concern to the ultimate goal of the entire cosmos. "Now," the father gently chided, "look how you mistreated so absent-mindedly the Almighty's creation. He formed it with purpose and gave it a Divine spark! It has its own self and its own life! Now tell me, how is the 'I am' of the leaf any less than your own 'I am'?"[1]

The same G-D who created the Heaven and Earth, the same G-D who created us, created every leaf, every tree. Every part that we see in this world has a purpose, and as we study the tree, we see the incredible purpose that each part of it provides for us in a supernatural way.

As we look to G-D's Word for the significance of the leaf, G-D coveys two very clear messages through the leaf. The leaf is not only a sign of prosperity, but it is also a sign of the times. Psalm 1:3 says, *"He is like a tree planted by streams of water, which yields its fruit in season and whose leaf does not wither. Whatever he does prospers."* And in Proverbs 11:28 we read, *"Whoever trusts in his riches will fall, but the righteous will thrive like a green leaf."*

We see that a green leaf is an indicator of new life and vitality. It is green because of the time of year and the right amount of water and light. It is green early in its life cycle, and in its green state it is soft, resilient, and full of life. The dry leaf is almost any color other than green. In some cases, it is robed in majestic colors, signifying its usefulness in life is about to end. For everything there is a season (see Eccles. 3:1-8).

Something as simple as a leaf can bear the good news of new life. Through an olive leaf, G-D gave Noah a simple sign of life so that that he would know that the waters had receded (see Gen. 8:6-11). Noah had confirmation that the trees had come forth on the Earth and in this season were now producing leaves.

In the New Testament, leaves also figure as signs of the times. In Luke 21:29-36, Yeshua tells His disciples a parable of the fig tree and its leaves:

> *Look at the fig tree and all the trees. As soon as they sprout their leaves, you see it and you know at once that summer is near. So also, when you see these all these things happening, know that the kingdom of G-D is near. Amen, I tell you, this generation will not pass*

away until all these things happen. Heaven and earth will pass away, but My words will never pass away.

But watch out so your hearts are not weighed down by carousing, strong drink, and the worries of life. Do not let that day come upon you suddenly like a trap. For it will come rushing upon all who live on the face of the whole earth. But stay alert at all times, praying that you may have the strength to escape all these things about to happen, and to stand before the Son of Man.

We tend to limit our understanding of the leaf and relegate it to a lowly position on the tree. To the untrained eye, it is only good for looking at in the fall and for signifying when spring is here. The leaf that we curse every fall when we rake our yards into mounds of waste, sacrifices its own life to return to the ground. In its death, it brings nourishment to the earth. In its death, it supports the one that brought it to life.

When we don't see the signs of the times—when we only look at the tree in its full glory, when it is full and lush, when the leaves change colors with the seasons—we miss G-D's message of new life, prosperity, good news, and His timetable. We take trips to the mountains to see how beautiful the trees are, and then for six months we ignore them. We drive past them, but even then G-D is speaking to us.

As we look at the leaf, we are reminded again of the parable the Lord spoke to my heart:

The children of the Kingdom of G-D are like the trees where the seasons change the outward appearance, but the root never changes. In its season, people gaze upon the buds and marvel at the branches. In its season, the colors like Joseph's robe burst forth, and people stand in awe. And winter comes, and the trees shed their beautiful leaves, and their outward appearance becomes bleak and barren. There's no longer any interest in the tree. But beneath the surface, the root grows deeper—yet no one sees.

When the bud comes forward and the leaf comes into fullness, we know that spring is upon us. Why then must we have blinders on our eyes about the current signs of the times? G-D gives us the signs of the times. He tells us that He is coming soon. He tells us to keep our eyes glued on Israel. He tells us to watch Jerusalem so we may know what is happening in G-D's economy.

Now learn the parable from the fig tree. When its branch becomes tender and puts forth leaves, you know that summer is near. So also, when you see all these things happening, know that it is near, at the door. Amen, I tell you, this generation will not pass away until all these things happen. Heaven and earth will pass away, but My words will never pass away (Mark 13:28-31).

SEVEN LESSONS LEARNED FROM THE LEAVES

1. The leaves turn toward the light for all nourishment, but it is not enough for just one leaf to turn to light. It requires all the leaves working in unity to gain the most benefit from the light. So too we must turn to light for our nourishment. *"And G-D said, 'Let there be light,' and there was light. G-D saw that the light was good, and He separated the light from the darkness"* (Gen. 1:3-4). In John 9:5, Yeshua declared, *"While I am in the world, I am the light of*

the world." Our eyes must be fixed on Yeshua, our Source of light.

2. Leaves give back as much as they receive. They take in carbon dioxide, and they release oxygen for us to live. Without the trees, we could not live. We could not breathe. We are also encouraged to give back cheerfully. *"Give to everyone who asks you; and whoever takes something of yours, make no demands upon him. Do to others as you would have them do to you"* (Luke 6:30-31).

3. When a leaf dies, it does not die in vain. The nutrients from its body are poured back into the tree. It invests itself in the next generation. We must be sure that we also invest in the next generations, for we are a source of light to them in what we give of ourselves. We are to be like the tree and return what has been given to us through wisdom, patience, understanding, and opportunity.

4. When a leaf dies, it brings life to another. Just as Yeshua died to bring life to us all, we must die to ourselves to bring forth new life in Messiah.

    Therefore if anyone is in Messiah, he is a new creation. The old things have passed away; behold, all things have become new" (2 Cor. 5:17).

    With respect to your former lifestyle, you are to lay aside the old self corrupted by its

*deceitful desires, be renewed in the spirit of
your mind, and put on the new self—created
to be like G-D in true righteousness and holiness* (Eph. 4:22-24).

5. What could be poisonous to us is life to the leaf.
    Carbon dioxide is poisonous to us in large doses.
    But this same gas is life for the leaf; and in His in-
    finite wisdom, G-D has created perfect balance.
    We are also to strive for balance in our lives. Too
    much of a good thing can become toxic and in the
    natural can cause an overdose or an imbalance.
    Rabbi Shaul said it best, "All things are lawful,
    but not all things are beneficial" (see 1 Cor. 10:23).

6. The leaf is a sign of the times; it comes forth in
    the spring and withers and falls in autumn. To
    everything there is a season. We cannot stop
    the seasons from arriving, but we can read the
    signs of the times and prepare ourselves accord-
    ingly. How foolish we are to resist change. How
    foolish we are to try to stop winter from com-
    ing because we love the fall so much. How fool-
    ish we are that we resist the winds of change.
    When we began to study the tree, I asked you:
    Are you an oak? Are you a palm tree? Will you
    stand so fixed and firm and rigid, yet so majes-
    tic and beautiful, that when the winds of change
    come you will either be uprooted or broken? Or,
    will you be like the palm tree, not so majestic
    kind of tall and scrawny looking, but when the
    winds of change come and blow, you bend and

conform to that change? The palm doesn't resist wind; it moves with it. And rather than foolishly being uprooted or broken, it goes with the change and survives.

7. The leaf is delicate in the spring, hardy in the summer, and dried and withered in the winter. Its end is made clear from its beginning as it is part of G-D's cycle of life. From its beginnings until its last days, it does not worry or fear for what is to come, but it is faithful to endure even in its death. If we are in right relationship with G-D, we too can endure even unto death without fear or worry—and in the death to ourselves receive life in Him.

LETTING GO

The lessons learned from the leaf are powerful. Something so small and insignificant as a bud on a branch of a tree can grow into something noteworthy. We are to use the leaf as our example. The leaf becomes a leaf when it's too painful for it to remain as a bud. Change will take place. For many, changes come whether they like it or not. Even unto death we are to embrace the gift that G-D has given us, for He endured even unto death so that in His death there would be life. Like the tree, we too must give back as much if not more than we receive. Neither the leaf nor the tree it grows on has control over its own life. Who of us can make even a hair on our head grow? Who of us can make a flower come forth out of nothing? Who of us can breathe life into dirt and create man? Like the leaf and the tree, we are helpless without G-D.

G-D is pulling at your heart strings; He is wooing you; and He is saying, "Come forth; it's too painful for you to remain as a bud." Life as you know it is not life as He wants it. Like the leaf, we must die to ourselves so that we may receive life. We only receive life through saying, "yes" to Yeshua, the promised Messiah. Say, "Lord I'm sorry. I'm sorry I've sinned against You, and I believe that Yeshua died for my sins. On the third day He rose again, and now He's sitting at the right hand of G-D interceding for me. Because He lives, I can live."

BURSTING FORTH

1. While in prison, Paul wrote, *"My G-D will fulfill every need of yours according to the riches of His glory in Messiah Yeshua"* (Phil. 4:19). Picture yourself as Paul in a Roman prison with lions devouring men somewhere outside the window. Hear the roars and screams. Now forget all that and reach out toward the only One who can supply all your needs. Sing the praises of Adonai and write letters of encouragement and love to others. Can you easily picture yourself being selfless in this situation? Or do you want to call anyone who you think may help you: family, friend, or lawyer? Think about a hard situation you have lived through. Now, write how your attitude and your actions were affected. Would you do things differently? Give some examples of what you will do and how you will act when tribulation hits again.

---

2. How do those closest to you describe you? Ask a few close family members, friends, or co-workers to tell you what they see in you and why. Do their ideas line up with that of a godly man

or woman? Should you change the way others perceive you? List the actions you can take to bring what you think others see in you and what others actually see in you into alignment.

_____

_____

_____

3. What investments have you made in your lifetime? Have you had a good return on those investments? The children or young adults around you make the best investment. List five ideals you desire to pass to the next generation.

_____

_____

_____

4. Incorporate new ways into your daily routine of living self-lessly. Turn your errands into self-sacrificing tasks: Purchase an extra little something for another when you load your grocery cart. House extra change in your pocket and in your car to give to those who ask. Create a box or container to collect small gifts for blessing someone randomly and without occasion. Restock your greeting cards to send to those who are shut-in or recovering. Fill your pockets with age-appropriate notions to give away to children at every Shabbat or service. Produce a business-card-sized blessing or Scripture designed to brighten someone's day. List five new activities to incorporate into your daily life that are selfless.

_____

_____

_____

5. Rate your lifestyle on a scale of 0–10:

Sleeps well:	1 2 3 4 5 6 7 8 9 10
Relaxes enough:	1 2 3 4 5 6 7 8 9 10
Laughs regularly:	1 2 3 4 5 6 7 8 9 10
Plays sometimes:	1 2 3 4 5 6 7 8 9 10
Enjoys life:	1 2 3 4 5 6 7 8 9 10
Gives joy to everyone:	1 2 3 4 5 6 7 8 9 10
Has no worries:	1 2 3 4 5 6 7 8 9 10
Sees beauty everywhere:	1 2 3 4 5 6 7 8 9 10
Has no fears:	1 2 3 4 5 6 7 8 9 10
Prays often:	1 2 3 4 5 6 7 8 9 10

Over the next 30 days, set goals for each score and work toward raising your scores until you feel you have more balance. Next month, take this test again and continue onward toward your set goal. We are in balance with what we were created for when we are unafraid, flowing in all the spiritual fruit (see Gal. 5:22), and when we have a healthy outlook on G-D's creation.

6. Are you uncomfortable with change? What do you dislike about it? For this exercise, wait until change comes. Then embrace it by having a bright outlook that all will work for good (see Rom. 8:28). Welcome and look forward to change, and in this way you will bend like the palm tree and not break like the mighty oak against a strong wind.

7. What season are you in? Some rate the seasons of life by age. Others categorize life seasons by the stages of the family. G-D sees our spiritual maturity in stages from childhood to mature adult. Do you imagine He sees you as a mature adult or as a child who only desires milk (see 1 Pet. 2:2)? Craving milk is a stage of early childhood. A child reads the Bible but does not apply what is read. A spiritual teenager may or may not crave milk but gets distracted with junk food. A less mature believer craves meat but is distracted with the doctrine of man. Those well-established in the Word crave only His Word, a deeper relationship with G-D, and a great desire to pass their love of G-D to others and to the next generation. Which stage are you in? Explain how you can maintain or move forward to a mature adult stage.

ENDNOTE

1. See http://www.chabad.org/library/articlecdo/aid/45561/
    jewish/Purpose-of-a-Leaf.htm; accessed January 26, 2012.

THE FRUIT

Chapter 7

THE FRUIT

THE FINAL STEP ON our journey takes us not only to the fruit of the tree, but also to the very basis for our assessment as to whether the tree is good or not. All trees that bear fruit flower, but not all flowering trees bear fruit. Some fruit-bearing trees have flowers that are self-pollinating, while others require both male and female trees to be in close enough proximity to each other that the male tree's pollen can be transferred to the female fruit-bearing tree. In order for the fruit to come forth, the flower must wilt and die.

Fruit is defined as the ripened seed-bearing part of a plant that is fleshy and edible. Simply stated, a fruit is any fleshy material covering a seed or seeds. Most fruits, from a horticultural perspective, are grown on a woody plant with the exception of strawberries. In other words, generally a fruit is the edible part of the plant that contains the seeds. So eggplant, tomato, cucumbers, and zucchini are all fruit.

The Hebrew word for fruit is one you may hear every Shabbat. Do you know it? *P'ree.* As in the blessing over the *Kiddish* when we drink the wine and we say, *"Baruch atah Adonai elohenu melech hoalam boray p'ree hagafen. Blessed art Thou oh Lord our G-D, King of the Universe who creates the fruit of the vine."* This is the same prayer said at the Passover Seder and the same prayer said over the wine or grape juice served in commemoration of the cup of Sanctification, the third cup lifted up for communion. Yeshua said He was the vine; therefore, it would make sense when He declared that the fruit of the vine was His blood of the New Covenant. Squeeze a grape and you get grape juice or wine. Squeeze a person and you get blood—symbolically, of course.

In the Garden of Eden both trees bore fruit:

> *The Lord G-D took the man and put him in the Garden of Eden to work it and take care of it. And the Lord G-D commanded the man, "You are free to eat from any tree in the garden; but you must not eat from the tree of the knowledge of good and evil, for when you eat of it you will surely die"* (Gen. 2:15-17).

One tree G-D told us to eat from for its fruit was good and provided life, and the other tree was forbidden by G-D as it held the keys to the knowledge of both good and evil.

Even today there are fruits that are beneficial and others that are poisonous. In G-D's perfect design, the seeds of different fruits can be swallowed whole by animals, remain undigested, and then be distributed to propagate new trees. In the natural, common seeds from certain fruits are toxic to humans and in quantity can be quite poisonous. The apple seed, if chewed, and the cherry pit are two common examples of potentially dangerous seeds that are housed in beneficial fruits.

Fruit must have time to mature and ripen. It requires examination on a number of levels to determine the optimum time of readiness. We go to the grocery store, stand there in the produce department, take the fruit—and what do we do? We become fruit inspectors. We feel it; we examine it for blemishes and for bruises; and often we smell it. Upon examination, we determine whether or not it's ripe and suitable to eat.

> *Either make the tree good and its fruit good, or make the tree rotten and its fruit rotten; for the tree is known by its fruit. You brood of vipers! How can you who are evil say anything good? For from the overflow of the heart the mouth speaks. The good man from his good treasury brings forth good, and the evil man from his evil treasury brings forth evil. But I tell you that on the Day of Judgment, men will give account for every careless word they speak. For by your words you will be justified, and by your words you will be condemned* (Matt. 12:33-37).

In the same way we inspect fruit in the produce section, we are to inspect the fruit of the people with whom we associate. The Word instructs us not to judge, but at same time it instructs us to be fruit inspectors. If we are to judge a tree by its fruit, we are also to examine the fruit in our own lives and the fruit produced by others.

Fruit, which is not picked in time, will rot on the tree and invite disease and insects to the tree or it will fall to the ground and be eaten by animals; or if the animals and the insects do not devour it, the produce will decay, break down, and nourish the ground. There is no waste in G-D's economy.

It is interesting to note that the word *p'ree,* fruit in Hebrew, may also refer to the offspring of animals or humans and the consequences of one's actions. That is to say, you are known by your words and your deeds.

We see this in G-D's Word in Psalm 92:12-15 and Psalm 128:1-4:

The righteous will flourish like a palm tree, they will grow like a cedar of Lebanon; planted in the house of the Lord, they will flourish in the courts of our G-D. They will still bear fruit in old age, they will stay fresh and green, proclaiming, "The Lord is upright; He is my rock, and there is no wickedness in Him."

Blessed are all who fear the Lord, who walk in His ways. You will eat the fruit of your labor; blessings and prosperity will be yours. Your wife will be like a fruitful vine within your house; your sons will be like olive shoots around your table. Thus is the man blessed who fears the Lord.

And in Proverbs 11:30, the same is true, *"The fruit of the righteous is a tree of life* [Etz Chaim], *and he who wins souls is wise."* Bearing fruit is important to G-D and to the building of His Kingdom. We read the instruction Yeshua gives us in John 15:9-17:

Just as the Father has loved Me, I also have loved you. Abide in My love! If you keep My commandments, you will abide in My love, just as I have kept My Father's commandments and abide in His love. These things I have spoken to you so that My joy may be in you, and your joy may be full.

This is My commandment, that you love one another just as I have loved you. No one has greater love than this: that he lay down his life for his friends. You are My friends if you do what I command you.

I am no longer calling you servants, for the servant does not know what his master is doing. Now I have called you friends, because everything I have heard from My Father I have made known to you.

You did not choose Me, but I chose you. I selected you so that you would go and produce fruit, and your fruit would remain. Then the Father will give you whatever you ask in My name.

These things I command you, so that you may love one another.

G-D's key to bearing fruit is rooted in love. Just as His instruction states–I have appointed you to go and bear fruit, fruit that will last and the Father will give whatever you ask in My name. This is My command for you to love each other.

G-D expands on one aspect of the fruit as defined in this passage:

Love is patient, love is kind, it does not envy, it does not brag, it is not puffed up, it does not behave inappropriately, it does not seek its own way, it is not provoked, it keeps no account of wrong, it does not rejoice over injustice but rejoices in the truth; it bears all things, it believes all things, it hopes all things, it endures all things (1 Cor. 13:4-7).

Patient. Kind. Longsuffering. Hope. Sound familiar? These and more make up the various parts of the fruit. Galatians 5:22-25 says:

But the fruit of the Spirit is love, joy, peace, patience, kindness, goodness, faithfulness, gentleness, and self-control—against such things there is no law. Now those who belong to Messiah have crucified the flesh with its passions and desires.

If we live by the Spirit, let us also walk by the Spirit.

The fruit of the Spirit is one fruit. And the key to all love is contained in that one fruit. Many people say "the fruits" of the Spirit. However, it's "the fruit" of the Spirit. There is one fruit, which is the evidence of the Spirit operating in us. There is a direct connection between the attributes of love in First Corinthians 13 and the fruit of the Spirit. For without the fruit of the Spirit, we cannot fulfill what Yeshua told us of the two greatest commandments: *"To love the Lord and to love your neighbor as yourself."* Take First Corinthians 13 and Galatians 5:22-23; map them over each other, and you'll see that the key to all is love. For us to bear fruit in G-D's economy, we must have captured this love. The Spirit must operate in us for us to even resemble G-D's love.

Each person must look at the fruit in his or her life. Is it ripe and flavorful, or hard and bitter? This fruit of the Spirit is one fruit made up of nine parts. No part can operate independently of the others, but all must work in the perfect harmony and balance that G-D breathed into you through the *Ruach HaKodesh*, the Holy Spirit: one fruit, nine parts. Like the compound unity of G-D, there is a compound unity of the fruit of the Spirit.

In Revelation 22:1-7, we read:

> *Then the angel showed me a river of the water of life—bright as crystal, flowing from the throne of G-D and of the Lamb down the middle of the city's street. On either side of the river was a tree of life, bearing twelve kinds of fruit, yielding its fruit each month; and the leaves of the tree were for the healing of the nations. No longer*

will be there be any curse. The throne of G-D and of the Lamb shall be in the city, and His servants shall serve Him. They shall see His face, and His name shall be on their foreheads. Night shall be no more, and people will have no need for lamplight or sunlight—for ADONAI Elohim will shine on them. And they shall reign forever and ever!

He said to me, "These words are trustworthy and true! ADONAI, the G-D of the spirits of the prophets, has sent His angel to show His servants what must happen soon. Behold, I am coming soon! How fortunate is the one who keeps the words of the prophecy of this book."

On each side of the river was the Tree of Life. No longer the Tree of the Knowledge of Good and Evil, for that curse was defeated in Messiah. Now, the *Etz Chaim*, the Tree of Life, the living Word of G-D, lines both sides of the river that we might receive nourishment each and every month as the 12 tribes of Israel—as the 12 gates to Jerusalem are swung open and *access to all is guaranteed.*

SEVEN LESSONS LEARNED FROM THE FRUIT

1. The sweetest fruit has allowed the heat of the day and the rain of the storm to soften its flesh so that it may ripen all the way through. So, too, we must allow the heat of the trials and the rain of the storms to soften our flesh all the way to our hearts so that we may be filled with His sweetness. It is through perseverance that our faith is strengthened, so that we are better equipped

to help others as they weather the elements in their lives.

2. Good trees bear good fruit. A bad tree cannot bear good fruit. It is only the Lord who can take a bad tree and make it good. This can only happen through a personal relationship with the very One who can transform us. We are to judge a tree and a person by the fruit according to the Word of G-D. We are instructed to be fruit inspectors.

3. Just as an apple is made up of parts—skin, flesh, core, stem, and seeds—the fruit of the Spirit is also made up of nine parts, all part of one fruit. It must be in full operation in us at all times in order for us to be nourished and for us to nourish one another. It is the sum of the parts that presents the whole picture of Messiah operating within us. It is the fruit of the Spirit that demonstrates that the Spirit is active within us. This is what provokes others to envy (see Rom. 11:11).

4. Fruit must be harvested when it is ripe. We must be sensitive to timing—for timing, even in nature, is everything. We must be sensitive to the needs of others and choose our timing wisely so that the harvest we reap is a bountiful one. The same fruit that is sweet when it is ripe is also quite bitter when eaten before its time. It is not sweet because the sugars are not perfected and the nutrients are not fully developed. In the same way that not getting all your nutrients contributes to

physical malnutrition, consuming only part of G-D's Word will cause spiritual malnutrition.

5. Fruit picked from the same tree does not all taste the same, but that does not condemn the entire tree. Like the apple seeds and the cherry pit, we must learn to take the good with the bad. No one is perfect, and we are not to judge unless we are willing to be judged by the same standard. Under the law, we have the right to focus on the bad and to seek damages; but under the law of grace, we have the option and obligation to forgive.

6. Fruit is the fleshly covering that holds the seeds inside. We are also to be like the fruit, sweet and firm, filled with seeds of life to plant in every person we meet. Our value is what is inside us and not our outward appearance. Man looks at the outward appearance, but G-D looks at the heart (see Gal. 2:6). It is what comes out of our hearts, through our words and our deeds, that brings about change in others.

7. The bearing of fruit proclaims the end of one cycle for the tree and the beginning of the next cycle all at the same time. In its own way, fruit is the Alpha and the Omega, the Aleph and the Tov, for that tree at that time. So too we see the Lord, who is the Beginning and the End; all life is contained in Him. The fruit of the tree is a sign that the end of the season has come, but when it falls to the

ground and its seed is replanted, it starts the process all over again.

THE HARVEST

Are you bearing fruit in your life? The Word of G-D says,
"Every branch that does not bear fruit will be cut off and
thrown into the fire" (see John 15:6). Every branch that does not
bear fruit is cut off and destroyed in G-D's Kingdom. To not
bear fruit also speaks to those who do not operate in the Spirit
to bring about the harvest for the Lord and to those who do not
love one another as G-D has loved them.

The v'ahavta from Deuteronomy 6:5 begins, *"Love the Lord
your G-D with all your heart and with all your soul and with all your
strength."* And in verses 6 and 7 it continues, *"These commandments that I give you today..."*—not yesterday, but today—*"...are
to be upon your hearts. Impress them on your children. Talk about
them when you sit at home and when you walk along the road, when
you lie down and when you get up."*

In Matthew 22:36-39, Yeshua was asked, "What are the two
greatest commandments?" He answered, v'ahavta:

> *"You shall love ADONAI your G-D with all your heart,
> and with all your soul, and with all your mind.' This is
> the first and greatest commandment. And the second is
> like it, 'You shall love your neighbor as yourself.'"*

Unless the fruit of the Spirit is fully operational in you, you
cannot love—for as we look at the definition of love, we see it
has all the attributes of the fruit of the Spirit. The key to unlock-
ing love is that G-D's Spirit must be operating in us.

Who of us can really love another as G-D intends us to
love? Others make you mad one minute; and then make you

happy the next. They're the greatest thing in the world; they're the worst thing in the world. I can't live with you; I can't live without you. Who of us can operate in that kind of unconditional love that G-D charges us with, unless we have the Spirit fully operating in us?

The fruit of the Spirit must be fully activated and operational. All of the fruit must be working together in perfect unity. One of nine, two of nine, seven of nine, eight of nine are still but a fraction of the one fruit. We must allow that fruit to ripen and mature in us for us to really understand that loving one another is more than giving the shirt off your back. Loving others is laying down your life for them. Loving another is esteeming that person more than yourself. This is evidence of the fruit of the Spirit operating in you.

The fruit is the end of one cycle and the beginning of the next. As the flower comes upon the tree, we gaze in wonder at the beauty of it. We look inside that flower and see the fruit begin to ripen; it comes forth hard and bitter in the beginning, but as it matures and ripens over time, sweetness emerges. G-D does a supernatural work, and the sugar begins to come out. Because of the heat of the sun and the light of the day, the rich goodness comes forth all in His time. Not every piece of fruit on the tree or the vine ripens precisely at the same time. Some fruit ripens early, and some ripens late. As the last piece of fruit is taken from the tree, the tree then begins to shut down, for the fall is coming. The tree knows that it cannot resist the change of the season, but it can prepare itself for the next season.

And so it is as we learn these lessons from the tree, we must be prepared for the next seasons of our lives. In this season, we are to bear fruit. Each one of us is to bear fruit. Luke 10:2 says, *"The harvest is plentiful, but the workers are few."*

Now is the time.

You are the one.

This is the place.

This is your time. This is your place, and you are the one for this season, the harvest season. Any branch that does not bear fruit is cut off and thrown into the fire. But every tree that brings forth fruit, that produces fruit, is pruned by G-D to bring an even greater harvest. If you're not growing like the tree, you're dying. If you're not bearing fruit, you're dying. Whether or not you're physically, emotionally, or spiritually dying, if you're not growing in the Lord, if you're not hungering and thirsting for more of Him and for less of you, you've missed it. Bear the fruit of love all the time and in all aspects of your life, and then you will not miss all the fullness that the Lord has for you in this life.

If you are reading this book and you are in sin, G-D cannot see your face. G-D can only see the back of your head as you walk away from Him, and He says He wants you to do an about-face so He can see you face to face. Just as the leaves of the tree turn themselves toward the sun, like the branches grow toward the light, we too must grow toward the Son, the Source of all light.

Holy fruit only comes from one place. Access to the Holy of Holies may be granted to all, but the Word of G-D says that no one comes to the Father but through the Son. You can stand outside and look, but the only way to make entrance in is through the Son, through Yeshua, our Messiah. John the Baptist said, "One will come after me even greater than I, one you do not know" (see Matt. 3:11). And as Yeshua Himself came up out of the water, the Spirit lit upon Him, accessible to all.

In Acts 2 we read that the Spirit is now available to all for the asking—but you must ask. You must invite Yeshua into your life.

You must invite Yeshua into your heart. There must be a change of season in your life, and the old must die so the new can appear. You say, "Rabbi, how do I do that?" Well, you say a simple prayer. It goes like this: "Lord, I'm sorry. I'm sorry I've sinned against You. I believe Yeshua died for my sins, and on the third day He rose again, and because He is sitting at the right hand of Your throne, Father, and because He lives, I can live today."

BEARING FRUIT

1. Love is patient, love is kind, it does not envy, it does not brag, it is not puffed up, it does not behave inappropriately, it does not seek its own way, it is not provoked, it keeps no account of wrong, it does not rejoice over injustice but rejoices in the truth; it bears all things, it believes all things, it hopes all things, it endures all things. Love never fails. Love is the sweetest fruit. May you burst forth in a tremendous harvest of the fruit of love. May it permeate every aspect of your life. May you always strive in all situations to share love with others. Walk in love all day, every day, and in every way.

_____

_____

_____

2. G-D is number one...period (see Exod. 20:3). Check all your priorities and ensure that each one lines up behind G-D. In this way, all your activities will be blessed. If I were forsaking the assembly by fishing on Shabbat or on the Lord's Day, then my priorities are not in order. If I tithed after taxes instead of on the gross, then my priorities are not in order. Then again, if I only attend service but barely give G-D a thought throughout the week, again, my priorities would not be in line with

His perfect order. List your out-of-order priorities and goals and repent; give them to G-D and drop any wrong inclinations.

_____

_____

_____

3. Take time and inspect the fruit of the Spirit inside you in the following matrix. Galatians 5:22-23 says, *"But the fruit of the Spirit is love, joy, peace, patience, kindness, goodness, faithfulness, gentleness, and self-control...."*

FRUIT INSPECTION (0–10)

Love:	1 2 3 4 5 6 7 8 9 10
Joy:	1 2 3 4 5 6 7 8 9 10
Peace:	1 2 3 4 5 6 7 8 9 10
Patience:	1 2 3 4 5 6 7 8 9 10
Kindness:	1 2 3 4 5 6 7 8 9 10
Goodness:	1 2 3 4 5 6 7 8 9 10
Faithfulness:	1 2 3 4 5 6 7 8 9 10
Gentleness:	1 2 3 4 5 6 7 8 9 10
Self-Control:	1 2 3 4 5 6 7 8 9 10

Where the fruit is below average (0–4), give some extra time to the care of this deprived fruit. Turn to G-D's Word to find examples and assistance, which you can then apply to your life. Ask others to help identify your withering fruit of the Spirit and take any suggestions they may offer for encouraging growth. Remember to pray and ask for counsel from the One who placed the fruit inside you. He, above all, knows what is lacking, and He knows what should be removed. Make a list of your wilted fruit. Beside each dehydrated fruit write a plan for nurturing it back to health.

_____

_____

_____

4. Refer again to the list in number 3. Is any of the fruit above average (7–10)? Harvest the 10s! When love is ready for reaping, it is as if Messiah Himself is moving and talking through you. It is the same with all other spiritual fruit. When Yeshua displays gentleness, part of the fruit of the Spirit, what does it look like? Answer this question for each part of the fruit of the Spirit. Then show others your best fruit of the Spirit.

_____

_____

_____

5. Many biblically based books have been written on the subject of love. We can love differently from others, and we can receive love diversely, too. Love may even have been developed despite surviving an unhealthy situation. Even cherries have pits! Remember, what was meant for harm, G-D intends

for good to accomplish what is now being done (see Gen. 50:20). Changing one thing in your past could mean that you never would have met Messiah Yeshua. Write a prayer of repentance, if necessary, for any regret you may feel for any situations in your past. Formulate and script blessings for each one who hurt you.

---

6. Psalm 34:8 says, *"Taste and see that the Lord is good."* Taste is the culmination of every environmental encounter over the lifetime of a fruit. If one aspect of the environment changes, then the entire taste of the fruit changes. Tasting fruit is also a way to inspect it. Does each part of your fruit of the Spirit taste good? Strive to have delectable and tasty fruit. Strive to be different in a variety of tastes. The sourness of lemons is great blended with different combinations of fruity flavors. If you are a bit sour in your personality, mix it in with the sweetness of another fruit. If you tend to be bland, add a little spice on occasion. Write a recipe that you think tastes good and determine how that plays out in your actions, comments, and personality.

---

7. There is a time for everything, and a season for every activity under Heaven (see Eccles. 3:1). When love dies, it is only for a season. When self-control is out of control, it is only for a season. When peace is overcome with a time of war, that too is only for a season. Whatever your season—good or bad—it is

destined to change. Remember, it's your attitude about your situation and not the situation itself that is measured and judged by the Lord and seen or tasted by others. Encourage someone today who is in a difficult season or experiencing a storm. Memorize five Scriptures of encouragement that you may hide in your heart for the difficult seasons of life.

_____

_____

_____

_____

_____

EPILOGUE

W HAT BEGAN IN A parable has taken us on a journey that started with the dirt and ended with fruit. The Lord spoke to me and gave me this parable:

> The children of the Kingdom of G-D are like the trees where the seasons change the outward appearance, but the root never changes. In its season, people gaze upon the buds and marvel at the branches. In its season, the colors like Joseph's robe burst forth, and people stand in awe. And winter comes, and the trees shed their beautiful leaves, and their outward appearance becomes bleak and barren. There's no longer any interest in the tree. But beneath the surface, the root grows deeper—yet no one sees.

The root in this parable is the Jewish root of the faith. For the past 2,000 years, the Jewish identity of the Messiah has been overshadowed by the birth and growth of the Gentile church. The plan and purpose of G-D was to continue to strengthen the root below the surface where no one could see so that its emergence would bring about the physical and spiritual restoration of Israel.

The parable that began this sermon series and ultimately this book parallels the dream and vision of Nebuchadnezzar and reveals to us the story of Israel. G-D raised up Israel, but its root is all that is left until Messiah returns. We know that the days are short; and through the reading of this section of the Book of Daniel, we are assured that the root is intact and awaiting for Messiah, our King, to return to restore Israel.

Read Daniel 4:4-37 with me:

> *I, Nebuchadnezzar, was at home in my palace, contented and prosperous. I had a dream that made me afraid. As I was lying in my bed, the images and visions that passed through my mind terrified me. So I commanded that all the wise men of Babylon be brought before me to inter-pret the dream for me. When the magicians, enchanters, astrologers and diviners came, I told them the dream, but they could not interpret it for me. Finally, Daniel came into my presence and I told him the dream. (He is called Belteshazzar, after the name of my G-D, and the spirit of the holy gods is in him.)*
>
> *I said, "Belteshazzar, chief of the magicians, I know that the spirit of the holy gods is in you, and no mystery is too difficult for you. Here is my dream; interpret it for me. These are the visions I saw while lying in my bed: I looked, and there before me stood a tree in the middle of the land. Its height was enormous. The tree grew large and strong and its top touched the sky; it was visible to the ends of the earth. Its leaves were beautiful, its fruit abundant, and on it was food for all. Under it the beasts of the field found shelter, and the birds of the air lived in its branches; from it every creature was fed.*
>
> *"In the visions I saw while lying in my bed, I looked, and there before me was a messenger, a holy one, coming down from heaven. He called in a loud voice: 'Cut down*

the tree and trim off its branches; strip off its leaves and scatter its fruit. Let the animals flee from under it and the birds from its branches. But let the stump and its roots, bound with iron and bronze, remain in the ground, in the grass of the field. Let him be drenched with the dew of heaven, and let him live with the animals among the plants of the earth. Let his mind be changed from that of a man and let him be given the mind of an animal, till seven times pass by for him.

"'The decision is announced by messengers, the holy ones declare the verdict, so that the living may know that the Most High is sovereign over the kingdoms of men and gives them to anyone he wishes and sets over them the lowliest of men.' "This is the dream that I, King Nebuchadnezzar, had. Now, Belteshazzar, tell me what it means, for none of the wise men in my kingdom can interpret it for me. But you can, because the spirit of the holy gods is in you."

Then Daniel (also called Belteshazzar) was greatly perplexed for a time, and his thoughts terrified him. So the king said, "Belteshazzar, do not let the dream or its meaning alarm you."

Belteshazzar answered, "My lord, if only the dream applied to your enemies and its meaning to your adversaries! The tree you saw, which grew large and strong, with its top touching the sky, visible to the whole earth, with beautiful leaves and abundant fruit, providing food for all, giving shelter to the beasts of the field, and having nesting places in its branches for the birds of the air—you, O king, are that tree! You have become great and strong; your greatness has grown until it reaches the sky, and your dominion extends to distant parts of the earth.

"You, O king, saw a messenger, a holy one, coming down from heaven and saying, 'Cut down the tree and destroy it, but leave the stump, bound with iron and bronze, in the grass of the field, while its roots remain in the ground. Let him be drenched with the dew of heaven; let him live like the wild animals, until seven times pass by for him.'

This is the interpretation, O king, and this is the decree the Most High has issued against my lord the king: You will be driven away from people and will live with the wild animals; you will eat grass like cattle and be drenched with the dew of heaven. Seven times will pass by for you until you acknowledge that the Most High is sovereign over the kingdoms of men and gives them to anyone He wishes. The command to leave the stump of the tree with its roots means that your kingdom will be restored to you when you acknowledge that Heaven rules. Therefore, O king, be pleased to accept my advice: Renounce your sins by doing what is right, and your wickedness by being kind to the oppressed. It may be that then your prosperity will continue."

All this happened to King Nebuchadnezzar. Twelve months later, as the king was walking on the roof of the royal palace of Babylon, he said, "Is not this the great Babylon I have built as the royal residence, by my mighty power and for the glory of my majesty?"

The words were still on his lips when a voice came from heaven, "This is what is decreed for you, King Nebuchadnezzar: Your royal authority has been taken from you. You will be driven away from people and will live with the wild animals; you will eat grass like cattle. Seven times will pass by for you until you acknowledge that the Most High is sovereign over the kingdoms of men and gives them to anyone He wishes."

Immediately what had been said about Nebuchadnezzar was fulfilled. He was driven away from people and ate grass like cattle. His body was drenched with the dew of heaven until his hair grew like the feathers of an eagle and his nails like the claws of a bird.

At the end of that time, I, Nebuchadnezzar, raised my eyes toward heaven, and my sanity was restored. Then I praised the Most High; I honored and glorified Him who lives forever. His dominion is an eternal dominion; His kingdom endures from generation to generation. All the peoples of the earth are regarded as nothing. He does as He pleases with the powers of heaven and the peoples of the earth. No one can hold back His hand and say to Him: "What have You done?"

At the same time that my sanity was restored, my honor and splendor were returned to me for the glory of my kingdom. My advisers and nobles sought me out, and I was restored to my throne and became even greater than before. Now I, Nebuchadnezzar, praise and exalt and glorify the King of heaven, because everything He does is right and all His ways are just. And those who walk in pride He is able to humble.

G-D shows us that in humility, repentance, and acknowledgement of His sovereignty, He will bring about the restoration of His Kingdom. He cuts off the high and lofty, but keeps the root strong and secure.

G-D has always preserved for Himself a remnant in order for the Messiah to return. And it is the role and calling of the Gentiles to provoke Israel to envy. Rabbi Shaul states, *"For if the Gentiles have shared in their spiritual blessings, they also ought to serve them in material blessings"* (Rom. 15:27).

This will be the sign for you, O Hezekiah: "This year you will eat what grows by itself, and the second year what springs from that. But in the third year sow and reap, plant vineyards and eat their fruit. Once more a remnant of the house of Judah will take root below and bear fruit above. For out of Jerusalem will come a remnant, and out of Mount Zion a band of survivors..." (2 Kings 19:29-31).

"I myself will gather the remnant of My flock out of all the countries where I have driven them and will bring them back to their pasture, where they will be fruitful and increase in number. I will place shepherds over them who will tend them, and they will no longer be afraid or terrified, nor will any be missing," declares the Lord. "The days are coming," declares the Lord, "when I will raise up to David a righteous Branch, a King who will reign wisely and do what is just and right in the land. In His days Judah will be saved and Israel will live in safety. This is the name by which He will be called: The Lord Our Righteousness.

So then, the days are coming," declares the Lord, "when people will no longer say, 'As surely as the Lord lives, who brought the Israelites up out of Egypt,' but they will say, 'As surely as the Lord lives, who brought the descendants of Israel up out of the land of the north and out of all the countries where He had banished them.' Then they will live in their own land" (Jer. 23:3-8).

Why is the restoration of Israel, the Olive Tree, so important? It is only through faith in Yeshua, the promised Jewish Messiah, that Israel will be restored and all of mankind redeemed. And the return of Yeshua requires that Jerusalem cries out, *"Baruch haba b'shem Adonai. Blessed is He who comes in the name of the Lord."*

O Jerusalem, Jerusalem who kills the prophets and stones those sent to her! How often I longed to gather your children together, as a hen gathers her chicks under her wings, but you were not willing! Look, your house is left to you desolate! For I tell you, you will never see Me again until you say, 'Baruch ha-ba b'shem ADONAI. Blessed is He who comes in the name of the LORD!"
(Matt. 23:37-39)

Upon Messiah's return, we see a beautiful picture of the Garden of Eden being restored and in the midst of all who believe. The vision of Heaven on Earth given is to be an encouragement to all that the promises of G-D are irrevocable. If He says He will do it, He will do it. The restoration of the Tree of Life is a fulfillment of G-D's plan for all mankind, that we would remain in His presence for eternity. This picture is made clear in these following passages:

*Then the angel showed me a river of the water of life—
bright as crystal, flowing from the throne of G-D and of
the Lamb down the middle of the city's street. On either
side of the river was a tree of life, bearing twelve kinds
of fruit, yielding its fruit each month; and the leaves of
the tree were for the healing of the nations. No longer
will be there be any curse. The throne of God and of the
Lamb shall be in the city, and His servants shall serve
Him. They shall see His face, and His name shall be on
their foreheads. Night shall be no more, and people will
have no need for lamplight or sunlight—for ADONAI
Elohim will shine on them. And they shall reign forever
and ever!*

*He said to me, "These words are trust- worthy and true!
ADONAI, the G-D of the spirits of the prophets, has
sent His angel to show His servants what must happen
soon. Behold, I am coming soon! How fortunate is the
one who keeps the words of the prophecy of this book."*

*I, John, am the one hearing and seeing these things. And
when I heard and saw them, I fell down to worship at the
feet of the angel showing me these things. But he tells me,
"See that you do not do that! I am a fellow servant with
you and your brothers the prophets and those keeping
the words of this book. Worship G-D!"*

*Then he tells me, "Do not seal up the words of the proph-
ecy of this book, for the time is near. Let the evildoer still
do evil, and the filthy still be filthy, and the righteous
still do righteousness, and the holy still be holy. Behold, I
am coming soon, and My reward is with Me, to pay back
each one according to his deeds.*

"I am the Alpha and the Omega, the First and the Last, the Beginning and the End. How fortunate are those who wash their robes, so that they may have the right to the Tree of Life and may enter through the gates into the city. Outside are the dogs and the sorcerers and the sexually immoral and the murderers and the idolaters, and everyone who loves and practices falsehood. I, Yeshua, have sent My angel to testify these things to you for My communities. I am the Root and the Offspring of David, the Bright and Morning Star."

The Spirit and the bride say, "Come!" And let the one who hears say, "Come!" Let the one who is thirsty come—let the one who wishes freely take the water of life! I testify to everyone who hears the words of the prophecy of this book. If anyone adds to them, G-D shall add to him the plagues that are written in this book; and if anyone takes away from the words of the book of this prophecy, G-D shall take away his share in the Tree of Life and the Holy City, which are written in this book.

The One giving testimony to these things says, "Yes! I am coming soon!" Amen! Come, Lord Yeshua! (Rev. 22:1-20).

Every journey has a beginning and an end. Each one of us must determine where our final destination will be. G-D has a plan for our lives. The plan is to never be separated from His love. The plan is to have our sins forgiven. The plan is for our atonement to be made for us so that what was once as red as scarlet can be made as white as snow. This plan was there in the beginning and was made clear when G-D separated the light from the dark and called the light good. Yeshua is the way. He is our Salvation; His very name, *Yeshua*, is the Hebrew word for Salvation.

> *This is what the Lord says: "Stand at the crossroads and look; ask for the ancient paths, ask where the good way is, and walk in it, and you will find rest for your souls..."* (Jer. 6:16).

Yeshua said:

> *Come to Me, all who are weary and burdened, and I will give you rest. Take My yoke upon you and learn from Me, for I am gentle and humble in heart, and 'you will find rest for your souls.' For My yoke is easy and My burden is light* (Matt 11:28-30).

> *There is salvation in no one else, for there is no other name under heaven given to mankind by which we must be saved* (Acts 4:12).

And in John 4:21-24, Yeshua declared:

> *Woman, believe Me, an hour is coming when you will worship the Father neither on this mountain nor in Jerusalem. You worship what you do not know; we worship what we know, for salvation is from the Jews. But an hour is coming - it is here now - when the true worshipers will worship the Father in Spirit and truth, for the Father is seeking such people as His worshipers. G-D is Spirit, and those who worship Him must worship in spirit and truth.*

CLOSING PRAYER

I₣ YOU HAVE COME to the end of this book and have yet to make a profession of faith in the promised Jewish Messiah, I want to ask you to please consider this passage:

> For G-D so loved the world that He gave His one and only Son, that whoever believes in Him shall not perish but have eternal life. G-D did not send the Son into the world to condemn the world, but in order that the world might be saved through Him. The one who believes in Him is not condemned; but whoever does not believe has been condemned already, because he has not put his trust in the name of the one and only Ben-Elohim.
>
> Now this is the judgement, that the light has come into the world and men loved the darkness instead of the light, because their deeds were evil. For everyone who does evil hates the light and does not come to the light, so that their deeds will not be exposed. But whoever practices the truth comes to the light, so that it may be made known that his deeds have been accomplished in G-D (John 3:16-21).

Please say yes to the One who came for you so that you can forever eat from the *Etz Chaim*—the Tree of Life. How do you say yes? Just say, "Lord, I am sorry I sinned against You, and I ask Yeshua into my heart. I believe He died for me and rose on the third day and is sitting at the right hand of G-D interceding for me. Because He lives, I can live now and forevermore. Amen."

Please e-mail me at bethhallel@bellsouth.net and share your decision or call my office at 205-822-2510 to ask any questions or share your decision.

GLOSSARY

Am Echad: one people; to dwell in unity

B'rit Hadasha: New Covenant, the Hebrew "New Testament"

Etz Chaim: Tree of Life

Hasatan: satan

HaShem: the Lord God; "the Name"

Kavannah: intentional preparation (of the heart); concentration

Lev Elohim: the Heart of G-D

Mishpacha: family, extended family

Mitzvot: commandments

P'ree: fruit

Rabbi Shaul: the apostle Paul

Ruach HaKodesh: Holy Spirit

Shaliach: apostle, emissary, agent

Shalom: peace, completeness, wholeness, health, safety

Shamishim: servants

Shlichim: apostles, sent ones

Talmadim: disciples

Tanakh: the Hebrew "Old Testament," including the Pentateuch, the psalms, and the prophets

tzelem Elohim: the image of God

V'ahavta: "And you shall love..."

Yeshua: Salvation in Hebrew, Jesus (Greek)

ABOUT THE AUTHOR

Rabbi Eric Walker is an ordained Messianic Jewish Rabbi. He is the Senior Rabbi of Congregation Beth Hallel in Birmingham, Alabama (www.shalombirmingham.com). He received his Jewish education from Rodef Shalom in Pittsburgh, Pennsylvania, and Temple B'nai Israel in McKeesport, Pennsylvania, and his undergraduate education at Penn State University. He has received continuing education in the Yeshiva Program under the International Association of Messianic Congregations and Synagogues (IAMCS) and at Messianic Conferences in connection with the Messianic Jewish Alliance of America (MJAA).

Rabbi Eric and his wife, Lora, have held a number of teaching and leadership positions at Congregation Beth Hallel in Roswell, Georgia, prior to planting Beth Hallel Birmingham in February 2007. Together they have raised two children in a home dedicated to the Jewish roots and heritage of their faith in Messiah Yeshua. Rabbi Eric is an Honorary Executive of the Messianic Jewish Alliance of America and is on the Board of Advisors of the Messianic Jewish Israel Fund.

Contact Information:
Congregation Beth Hallel
2230 Sumpter Street
Birmingham, AL 35226
Phone: 205-822-2510
E-mail: bethhallel@bellsouth.net

IN THE RIGHT HANDS, THIS BOOK WILL CHANGE LIVES!

Most of the people who need this message will not be looking for this book. To change their lives, you need to put a copy of this book in their hands.

> But others (seeds) fell into good ground, and brought forth fruit, some a hundred-fold, some sixty-fold, some thirty-fold (Matthew 13:8).

Our ministry is constantly seeking methods to find the good ground, the people who need this anointed message to change their lives. Will you help us reach these people?

> Remember this—a farmer who plants only a few seeds will get a small crop. But the one who plants generously will get a generous crop (2 Corinthians 9:6).

EXTEND THIS MINISTRY BY SOWING
3 BOOKS, 5 BOOKS, 10 BOOKS, OR MORE TODAY,
AND BECOME A LIFE CHANGER!

Thank you,

Don Nori Sr., Founder
Destiny Image
Since 1982

DESTINY IMAGE PUBLISHERS, INC.

"Promoting Inspired Lives."

VISIT OUR NEW SITE HOME AT
WWW.DESTINYIMAGE.COM

FREE SUBSCRIPTION TO DI NEWSLETTER

Receive free unpublished articles by top DI authors, exclusive discounts, and free downloads from our best and newest books.

Visit www.destinyimage.com to subscribe.

Write to: Destiny Image
             P.O. Box 310
             Shippensburg, PA 17257-0310

Call: 1-800-722-6774

Email: orders@destinyimage.com

For a complete list of our titles or to place an order
online, visit www.destinyimage.com.